W9-CTQ-782

where on EARTH...?

Introduction

Where on Earth Can I...? answers travel questions large and small. Divided into five chapters, it covers the natural landscape, best wildlife experiences, most spectacular buildings, and sights. There is also a section devoted to thrill-seeking (be it destinations for chocoholics, or wild-water rafting along the Amazon). The final chapter looks at ultimate vacation experiences, from palaces where you can bunk down for the night, to nostalgic dinners, trips to see Santa Claus, and even the chance to join the world's first space tourists.

Whether you are an avid adventurer or an armchair dreamer, this is your guide to a world of exciting journeys. Happy traveling!

Where on Earth...?

Libby Norman

METRO BOOKS
NEW YORK

© 2008 by New Holland Publishers (UK) Ltd

This 2008 edition published by Metro Books by arrangement with
New Holland Publishers (UK) Ltd.

All rights reserved. No part of this publication may be reproduced, stored
in a retrieval system, or transmitted, in any form or by any means, electronic,
mechanical, photocopying, recording, or otherwise, without prior written
permission from the publisher.

Copyright © in text: Libby Norman
Copyright © New Holland Publishers (UK) Ltd
Design by Sue Rose

ISBN-13: 978–1–4351–0331–3
ISBN-10: 1–4351–0331–9

Printed and bound in Singapore

10 9 8 7 6 5 4 3 2 1

The author of this work has asserted her moral right to be identified
as the author of this work.

The authors and publishers have made every effort to ensure that all information contained in this book was
correct at the time of press. They accept no responsibility for any loss, injury or inconvenience sustained by any
person using this book or the advice given within it.

Contents

CHAPTER 1

Natural Wonders

From the highest unclimbed mountain and the deepest canyon, to spectacular waterfalls, active volcanos, and thermal springs, this first chapter explores the diversity of our planet and highlights must-see heights, sights, and locations around the globe.

We've included living natural wonders— including the world's most prolific plant species— as well as notable giants, ancients, and oddities. You will also find a guide to great wilderness landscapes and unique ecosystems, along with some unsung natural treasures growing all around us.

Climb the world's highest mountain

Mount Everest on the Nepal-Tibet border is the world's loftiest mountain, standing 29,028ft (8,848m) high. It's still growing, too–rising a fraction a year because of shifting geology in the Himalayas.

Although it stands head and shoulders above the rest, Everest sits in the middle of high ground known as the Tibetan Plateau, so the actual distance from base to peak is a less awesome 12,000ft (3,700m).

This doesn't stop climbers from viewing this giant as the "must-climb" experience, or trekkers from enjoying the majestic Himalayan countryside. Indeed, the mountain summit where Edmund Hillary and Tenzing Norgay placed their flag in 1953 has been pretty crowded in succeeding decades. More than 2,200 people are recorded as having reached the summit—over half since 1998.

Each climber is typically expected to raise about $60,500 in sponsorship or from savings to pay for equipment, climbing costs, and government fees, making their achievement all the more impressive. These days it's hard to get your name in the record books unless you're prepared to join the ranks of the serious thrill-seekers who ski, paraglide, or land their helicopters near the summit in order to achieve that coveted first. Special credit should go to Nepalese climbers Moni Mulepati and Pem Dorjee Sherpa, who achieved the ultimate cloud-nine romantic experience by getting married on the summit in 2005. This must have been one of the shortest wedding receptions in history (about ten minutes), but the couple did briefly take off their oxygen masks to don garlands and exchange vows in front of their 45 guests, who were all part of a Nepalese Rotary Club centenary expedition.

View the loftiest unclimbed summit

Sometimes it's the things you can look at but not touch that are most appealing, and Gangkhar Puensum in the remote kingdom of Bhutan would certainly be on most mountaineers' 'to do' list.

While some visitors have claimed that the purity of Nepal's pristine white slopes has been wrecked by tourists, and the trash they leave behind in their bids to conquer Everest (see previous page), Bhutan remains almost as remote and magical a place as it was two centuries ago. The air is so pure that it is intoxicating. This is a country that has just one set of traffic lights—and this has been designed so it sits on top of a small Buddhist shrine. The kingdom of Bhutan's tourist policy has preserved this splendid isolation. Visitor numbers are strictly controlled and, once in the country, they can only travel with official tour guides on recognized and approved routes.

If you're lucky enough to make it into the country, you can take a variety of stunning trekking trails around lush valleys, visit remote villages, and view shrines and temples perched on the high cliffs and mountain ledges.

As for mighty Gangkhar Puensum's 22,895ft (7,541m) peak, it stands there just begging to be climbed. However, it is strictly off-limits, and will remain so for the foreseeable future. This is because mountain climbing was banned in this Himalayan kingdom in 2003 out of respect for the religious beliefs of its population who view the peaks as sacred. The mountain straddles the border with Tibet, and there is speculation that eventually the summit will be attempted from the other side of the border. But, for now at least, it remains virgin territory.

Experience a low point

The name Death Valley certainly doesn't sell this as a beauty spot, but this is a truly unique American wilderness with spectacular scenery. It is also one of the lowest, driest, and hottest points on the planet.

If the gaudy neon of the Vegas strip has left your wallet empty and your nerves jangling, head out to Death Valley to recharge your batteries.

This is life on the edge, a place where sometimes no rain falls for a whole year and the mercury rises to 120° fahrenheit (49° Celsius) on a routine summer's day. When it does rain, this dry and parched scenery can change almost in front of your eyes. More than 1,000 plant species thrive here—some have root systems ten times your height, others send out a shallow network of roots over a vast area to find nutrients. Visit in the spring and you may be rewarded with white desert star, vivid red Indian paintbrush, and lilac sunbonnet.

At Badwater—official lowest point at 282ft (86m) below sea level—you can take a trail out into the vast salt flats. At nearby Artist's Drive, the rocks have been stained different colors by minerals, while Devil's Golf Course is a lunar landscape of salt crystal balls. You can see amazing weathered canyons at Zabriskie Point, and admire sand dunes at Stovepipe Wells.

If you get tired of the harsh landscape, hike part of the way up through the forests of Telescope Peak. From its 11,049ft (3,368m) summit there's a vertical drop twice as deep as the Grand Canyon. A shorter (and easier) trail up Wildrose Peak offers you some of the best views of the valley below.

Explore great caves

There's a vast subterranean world below our feet that has barely been explored, so the record breakers we know about may just be small fry. Here are some majestic caves that are already on the map.

1. Cango Caves, South Africa
This Oudtshoorn attraction is famous for its wonderful rock formations. The most spectacular area, Van Zyl's Hall, has an organ pipe-style arrangement of stalactites.

2. Fingal's Cave, Scotland
You need to take a boat trip to view the inspiration for Mendelssohn's *Hebrides Overture*. Located on the uninhabited island of Staffa, its entrance is guarded by basalt columns giving it the look of a giant cathedral.

3. Grotte des Demoiselles, France
Close to Montpellier in the Thaurace mountains, this fairy grotto is full of giant stalactites, draperies, and cascades. The centerpiece is a calcite-rock formation that resembles the Virgin and Child. A funicular carries you up to the entrance of the cave.

4. Gunung Mulu, Borneo
This national park is home to extraordinary caves including Sarawak Chamber, currently the world's largest cave. You need to be an experienced caver to explore it, but novices can visit others in the system, including Clearwater and Lang's Caves.

5. Mammoth Cave, Kentucky
Part of a national park, this system is one of the best explored in the world—it's currently also the longest cave. You can take anything from self-guided tours, to history trails, and early-evening lantern tours.

THE SALT CATHEDRAL

One of the most beautiful man-made caves is Colombia's Catedral de Sal in Zipaquirá. Centuries-old salt mines had become so vast by the 1920s that they were converted into an eerie underground cathedral

See an arid tropical forest

We associate the tropics with rain forest, but they are also home to dry forests—arid biomes that are rich in unusual plants and flowers. One of the best reserves to visit is on the lush Caribbean island of Puerto Rico.

Forest and rain go together in the tropics, but dry broadleaf forests do exist, and these arid settings are home to plants and animals that have adapted to harsh conditions. One of the finest examples of this rare biosphere is El Bosque Estatal de Guánica in the far south of Puerto Rico. Covering an area of around 500 square miles (800sq km), this narrow strip is subjected to minimal rainfall and baking sun—a combination that produces unusual riches. You find scrub forest and semi-evergreens close to the coast, along with giant cacti, including the melon cactus, and the multi-stemmed variety known locally as "Spanish dildo." You also see trees with twisted, almost bonsai-like forms and thick trunks to hold water reserves.

Many of the 700 or so species found here are critically endangered, and it is the same story with the wildlife. Naturalists come in search of the crested toad, purple land crab, and Puerto Rican nightjar. You'll also find an endemic woodpecker, beautiful emerald hummingbird, and—if you're lucky—green and leatherback turtles. With over 35 miles (56km) of trails, and some of the least developed coastline on the island, this makes a great wilderness trek. If you feel like a complete contrast after this parched setting, head for the famous El Yunque reserve on the east of the island for lush greenery and plenty of cooling rain showers.

Scale the world's tallest sand dunes

Rising like a mountain above a sun-baked landscape, the dunes of the Namib Desert dwarf even those of Arabia. Bright orange sand, and the twisted stumps of long-dead trees create a surreal and magical landscape.

Lying within Namib-Naukluft National Park in Namibia, the sand dunes of Sossusvlei are an unforgettable sight—particularly after a long drive over bone-crunchingly bad roads from the capital Windhoek, or the coastal resort of Swakopmund. But it is worth the effort, particularly if you catch them at sunrise or sunset.

The peaks of the 984ft (300m) "sand mountains" have strange ridges sculpted by the strong winds that blow in from the Atlantic. This is a place where you want to immediately kick off your shoes and start climbing—although it can be a hard, uphill trek in searing heat; it is best to go in a group, making sure that you take plenty of water.

In the center of the sand dunes lies a huge clay pan that may only fill up with rain once in a decade. Despite this, you find a sparse sprinkling of greenery in places. However, in the area known as Dead Vlei, the gnarled stumps of long-dead trees sticking up through the sand are the only visible sign that life once went on here.

While this is an ancient landscape, it is not frozen in time— the winds are constantly reshaping the dunes' peaks, and creating strange patterns that look spectacular from a light aircraft.

FOUR MORE SURREAL DESERT LANDSCAPES

1. ATACAMA DESERT, CHILE

Officially the driest place on earth, this has areas where rain has never been known to fall, and much of the desert relies on the moisture from fog blowing off the Pacific. In a place packed full of weird vistas, the strangest of all is Valle de la Luna, a landscape of petrified plant and animal fossils, wind-eroded rocks, and the odd straggly tree clinging on for dear life.

2. DADES VALLEY, MOROCCO

With the High Atlas Mountains on one side, and Jbel Sarhro range on the other, this is a romantic desert landscape of looming ocher cliffs and ruined forts (kasbas), interspersed with ancient oases where dates and figs grow.

3. ORGAN PIPE CACTUS NATIONAL MONUMENT, ARIZONA

Right on the border with Mexico, this reserve in the Sonoran Desert is home to giant cactus plants and weird, arched rock formations, particularly photogenic if you take the Ajo Mountain Drive route.

4. WHITE SANDS NATIONAL MONUMENT, NEW MEXICO

Pure white gypsum sand rising from the Tularosa Basin has created amazing dune formations. This landsape can be experienced on foot (although follow safety advice from park guides) or by taking the scenic drive. You can even buy "snow saucers" at the visitor center and go sliding down the dunes.

Visit an ancient boreal landscape

We worry about the Amazon rain forest, but boreal forests, or taiga, are just as precious a natural resource, forming a continuous belt across Eurasia and North America to create the largest carbon sink on the planet.

The rain forests of the southern hemisphere may be lush and exotic, but the boreal forests at a latitude of about 70° degrees north create a vital green lung that is every bit as threatened by activities such as logging. This great Eurasian wilderness stretches from Sweden in the west to Siberia in the east, while in northern North America, the patch of green on the map covers a belt from the Pacific to Atlantic coasts.

Much of this is bear country, but it is also home to raptors and wolves and, in the far east, the rare Siberian tiger. It is inhospitable in winter, but in summer it can be warm and humid, with more than its fair share of biting insects. Typically, the tree canopy is a mixture of conifers and deciduous species such as birch and oak, and the fertile forest floor is rich in ferns and wild flowers. In Europe, one of the easiest places to experience boreal forest is Finland. Sparsely populated, it has national parks, and an open-access policy that makes it easy to go hiking. To see real wilderness, visit the taiga at Yugud-Va National Park in Russia's Komi Republic—the largest remaining expanse of ancient forest within Europe.

Residents of Canada don't have to travel so far. Around a quarter of the world's untouched or "virgin" woodland is here, and even residents of Ontario's towns and cities only have a journey of an hour or so before they can lose themselves in an ancient landscape.

Sit under an upside down tree

You won't get much shade under a baobab because it is thin on branches and leaves, but this ancient and curious tree is both the stuff of legends and a legendary survivor.

The species is native to Madagascar (it's also the national tree), but you'll find baobabs in tropical Africa and Australia, and a few introduced specimens survive in Mannar, Sri Lanka. The description of them as the "upside-down tree" comes from an Arabian legend that the Devil plucked the baobab from the ground and replanted it the wrong way up. It is easy to see how this story came about looking at the long, smooth trunk topped with strange, tufty branches that look very much like roots.

Despite its comical appearance, this tree is an amazing example of how living things are matched to their environment. The smooth trunk may not grow that tall, but its girth can be huge—up to 23ft (7m) has been recorded. This is its secret of survival, because the trunk is like a giant water tank, holding reserves to survive the dry season. In the rainy months, it grows its leaves, and then sprouts saucer-like white flowers that open at dusk, and are pollinated by fruit bats and insects. The fruit is highly prized by both humans and monkeys (its African name is monkey bread tree).

Generally the baobab grows in splendid isolation, but perhaps the best place to see them *en masse* is Madagascar. The Indian Ocean island is home to six indigenous species and even boasts Baobab Alley, an imposing avenue of these unusual trees near the town of Morondava.

Drive through a giant redwood

The most iconic of the "drive-through" redwoods was the Wawona Tree in Yosemite, California, which fell over in 1969, its giant 2,500-year-old frame unable to support the weight of a heavy snowfall.

Redwoods (sequoia) were among the earliest West Coast tourist attractions; canny landowners who had one of these giants on their land would carve a route through the tree for motorists who could then get their pictures taken. No one knows if Wawona's end was hastened by this treatment, but it probably didn't help.

Three famous drive-through redwoods remain. All are close to Route 101 and from south to north they begin with Leggett Chandelier Tree, which is around 190 miles (310km) north of San Francisco. Drive on to Eureka for Myers Flat Shrine Tree, and Klamath Tour Thru Tree. Both are on the appropriately named Avenue of the Giants. If you prefer to admire redwoods in their natural state, this is a good access point for Rockefeller Forest. You need to go farther still to Montgomery Woods State Reserve near the town of Ukiah to find what is reputed to be the world's tallest specimen: Mendocino Tree was measured at 367ft (112m) in 1999.

THE MIGHTY GENERAL

Mendocino Tree may be loftiest, but the far more famous General Sherman is classified as the largest because of the huge volume of its trunk. It's at Sequoia National Park, about an hour's drive from Visalia in California's San Joaquin Valley. General Sherman is in fact a giant redwood— a different species from the coast redwoods you find farther north. Its circumference is some 102ft (31m), so tree huggers will need to go in a group.

Take a treetop walk

The Valley of the Giants in Western Australia boasts one of the world's most spectacular treetop walks. Not for the faint-hearted, it takes you high into the canopy of giant eucalyptus trees.

If you don't mind extreme heights, or the feeling of being suspended in space on a wobbly bridge, then the treetop walk in Walpole-Nornalup National Park is for you. The park hugs the coast, near Denmark, and is famous for its majestic tingle trees, a species of giant eucalyptus that only grows in this region.

The treetop walk is unusual because rather than being a platform, it's built on a series of long trusses, designed to blend into the natural environment and move in response to footfall. The effect is a bit like standing on a wobbling branch, and as you are around 130ft (40m) in the air, this is about as close as you'll get to feeling like one of the local birds who inhabit the 200ft (60m) trees around you. Vertigo sufferers may prefer the forest floor boardwalk known as the Ancient Empire. Not only are your feet on solid ground, but you can also appreciate the huge girth (up to 80ft/24m), and hollowed-out centers of many of the older trees.

A BIRD'S EYE VIEW OF A NORTHERN WILDERNESS

🌳 Haliburton Forest in Ontario offers treetop walks through a pristine northern forest. This is highland country with a wolf reserve, great fishing, and mountain biking. The 65ft (20m) high treetop walk is through an area of giant white pines, and you are securely strapped into safety harnesses before you begin your climb.

Stay in a rainforest reserve

The best way to experience true rain forest wilderness is to get up close to it by camping in an eco-lodge. Lush Costa Rica offers some of the best back-to-nature locations on the planet.

Costa Rica has become a byword for eco-tourism, with lodges and cabins dotted around its tropical rain forests. Over a tenth of the country is national park, and almost a third is protected from activities such as logging and building development.

You are spoiled for choice when it comes to forest lodgings, but one of the most remote and spectacular settings is at Corcovado Lodge Tent Camp. Situated on the Osa Peninsula close to the border with Panama, it's a series of well-appointed tents sandwiched between the surf of the Pacific and Parque National de Corcovado. If you want pristine jungle, it's here, along with flocks of scarlet macaws, white-faced and howler monkeys, and poison-dart frogs. You may even find the trail of a jaguar or cougar.

One of the highlights here is to be hoisted 115ft (35m) into a guapinol tree to view the rain forest canopy. You can even elect to spend the night camping on the platform immersed in the sounds of the nocturnal jungle (and then woken up by a deafening dawn chorus).

RAIN FOREST LUXURY

For the ultimate luxury rain forest vacation, head for Chan Chich Lodge. Sited on Gallon Jug Estate north of Belize City, it sits in the middle of La Selva Maya, the largest continuous forest north of the Amazon basin. This is nirvana for birdwatchers, but also one of the best places to see jaguar, puma, and ocelot.

See a host of golden daffodils

The annual spring display of trumpet-shaped yellow flowers that inspired the Romantic poet William Wordsworth to wax so lyrical 200 years ago, is still a visitor attraction in the English Lake District.

You may not be "lonely as a cloud" if you visit Ullswater in March, since tourists trek by the thousands to witness the native *Narcissus pseudonarcissus* that inspired the great Romantic poet to write one of his most famous works "Daffodils." He is said to have been inspired during a walk around this Lake District beauty spot.

These are not the bold trumpets we are used to seeing in spring gardens, but a diminutive wild flower with pale yellow outer petals. Wordsworth described seeing 10,000 blooms at a glance, and the massed effect is certainly impressive today, although concern that larger hybrids are colonizing the area and may subsume the wild variety has lead to urgent preservation efforts in recent years.

Ullswater is easily accessible from Penrith, and you can take in the stunning views from Aira Force waterfall. It's also worth a visit to Wordsworth's favorite family home at Rydal Mount, overlooking Lake Windermere.

WALK THROUGH A BLUEBELL WOOD

While Britain's native daffodils may be under threat, bluebells are an even rarer sight. One of the best places to see a carpet of them in bloom is the Royal Horticultural Society's garden at Wisley, in Surrey. Here the woodland Bluebell Walks have become an annual institution. The typical flowering time is mid-May, although check ahead as late frosts can delay the show.

Become an orchid hunter

We may think of them as rare and exotic blooms, but orchids are the largest plant family, growing from the Arctic to Australia. Many species have developed unusual means of growing and reproducing.

The orchid has been prized through history for its fragrance and supposed aphrodisiac qualities. In the 19th century, plant collectors cut a swathe through many of its habitats in a desperate scramble to bring home new and ever more exquisite blooms. Money and fame awaited them if they found a choice variety. Today, the threat comes from activities such as logging and deforestation, but even so, around 250 new varieties are discovered each year, adding to a tally of around 25,000 species.

One of the most fascinating aspects of orchids is their variety. Some are epiphytes, anchored onto trees and shrubs from which they obtain moisture using aerial roots. Others thrive on unpromising rocky soil, obtaining nutrients from the atmosphere, and a third group requires dense woodland, feeding on decaying plant matter. There is even an underground variety in Australia that survives without light and is pollinated by ants.

What intrigues scientists is the seductive methods they use to attract pollinators to ensure reproduction. The lady's slipper leads insects down a passage into the flower, and the only route out is past the pollen. The bumblebee orchid replicates the pheromones of the female bumblebee, and male bumblebees get a liberal coating of pollen when they attempt to mate with the flower. Less appetizing is the bulbophyllum, which smells like a rotting carcass, and is pollinated by passing flies.

FIVE PLACES TO SEE ORCHIDS

1. LONDON

The hothouses of the Royal Botanic Gardens at Kew have one of the most diverse collections in the world. Many are grown from seed to be replanted in the wild, and Kew hosts a month-long orchid festival each February when you can see around 500,000 of them in bloom.

2. MADAGASCAR

This is a major commercial center for the vanilla orchid, used as flavoring and in perfumes. It grows as a vine, and you can see it in production and buy the finished product around the island.

3. MOYOBAMBA

The regional capital of San Martin, northern Peru, is known as the City of Orchids because over 3,000 species grow in the humid tropical landscape around it.

4. SINGAPORE

The National Orchid Garden at the country's botanical gardens boasts around 1,000 species and 2,000 hybrids, and includes a cool house to display species that grow in tropical highland areas.

5. TASMANIA

Warmer lowlands close to the coast are where you are most likely to spot wild orchids, but they have a tendency to crop up all over the place, and there are varieties in bloom just about every month of the year.

Visit more places famous for flowers

From the much-painted wild landscapes of Provence, to the formal beauty of Japanese gardens, here are five places that have captured the imagination of painters and travelers.

1. Keukenhof, the Netherlands

Holland is a riot of color in the spring, and the best place to see tulips (and daffodils and hyacinths) is Keukenhof Gardens in Lisse, a town between Amsterdam and the Hague. This festival lasts from late March to late May and attracts visitors from around the globe.

2. Pretoria, South Africa

Known as Jacaranda City, Pretoria turns purple around blossom time in October when more than 70,000 of the exotic trees come into full bloom. They are not native to the city—having been imported from South America—but the sight of fluffy mauve garlands lining the city's main thoroughfares is unforgettable.

3. Provence, France

From mid-June to the end of September, Provence's famous lavender fields are in bloom. You can take bus tours from Avignon, or rent a car and travel down through Apt and Sault.

4. Tokyo, Japan

Cherry blossom (sakura) is Japan's unofficial national flower, and the country is awash with blossom in mid-March. Blossom-viewing parties are a time-honored tradition and one of the best (and busiest) viewing spots is Shinjuku Gyoen National Garden, Tokyo, which has over 1,000 cherry trees.

5. Valencia, Spain

Surrounded by citrus groves, Valencia is not only the city of oranges but also of flowers. There are numerous parks and gardens, but if you want to see fragrant orange blossom, head to Jardín de las Hespérides which has more than 50 citrus varieties.

Watch nature's most spectacular fireworks show

Some things in this world are best viewed from a safe distance, and Kilauea on the island of Hawaii is definitely one of them. It's generally regarded as earth's most active volcano, and has been erupting non-stop since January 1983.

Fortunately for visitors, this is also one of the most easily accessible natural firework shows, and has been promoted as Hawaii's "Drive-in Volcano." Long lava flows are visible from a car or via a short walk, but perhaps the best views can be seen from the air on a helicopter tour. The best time to go is late afternoon, when the vibrant colors of lava flowing across lunar landscapes, or directly into the sea are set against that world-famous Hawaiian sunset.

Kilauea is the youngest of the island's volcanos, and sits in the shadow of the much larger Mauna Loa. But islanders have always known it must be treated with respect. Legend has it that it is home to Pele (the Hawaiian volcano goddess, not the soccer star), and its name translates as "spewing."

Most of Kilauea's summit is covered by vast quantities of ash laid down in a series of previous eruptions. In about 1790, an eruption is said to have effectively settled a tribal war when at least 80 warriors from one side were killed. In 1924, a column of ash was thrown two miles (3.2km) into the air, along with giant boulders. At times, day was turned into night in Pahala, the closest town downwind of the volcano.

Explore the garden of Eden

One of the most ambitious garden-creations ever devised, the Eden Project sprang to life from a disused quarry, and has brought the diversity of the world's ecosystems to an industrial corner of Cornwall.

It's a wonderful creation story, and one that has revived the tourist fortunes of a corner of Cornwall, as well as helping to foster a greater understanding of the value of plants, ecosystems, and diversity. Back in 1995, Bodelva was an old china-clay pit coming to the end of its working life, supplying raw materials to the pottery industry. It was also an almighty gray blot on the landscape, and plans were set up to reclaim the land. What the team behind the Eden Project realized, was that this gouged-out dip provided a sheltered spot where, given the right soil and conditions, plants could thrive.

So Eden was born, and when it finally opened in 2001, it contained over 5,000 plant species from around the globe. The most ambitious creation was the Tropics Biome—the largest conservatory in the world. Measuring 785ft by 380ft (240m by 110m), this giant bubble replicates the climate of the rain forest, and has become home to orchids, giant bamboo, cocoa, and coffee plants as well as luscious tropical bananas and mangos. The Warm Temperate Biome shows off the rich flora of the Mediterranean, South Africa, and California with citrus, grape vines, rare grains, and chilli peppers. Outside, a third Biome covers the temperate regions of the world, and includes everything from fields of lavender, to tea and hop plants. One side-benefit of this giant garden is that a once-sterile site is now teeming with fauna as well as flora. Butterflies, lizards, and other welcome wildlife colonize the jungle, the savanna, and the temperate zones. Some introduced species, including tree frogs, praying mantis, and tiny birds called Sulawesi White Eyes help to keep down pests in the Tropics Biome.

For visitors, this is a unique opportunity to see the rich diversity of plants in one place (it takes about four hours to cover the major regions of the globe). But the Eden Project also has a mission to explain the relationships between plants and man, telling a story that spans the history of crop cultivation and plants as medicine, but also covers the rise of supermarket imports, and the future of green fuels and sustainable farming. Although it was intended as a local tourist attraction, Eden has become a huge international hit, attracting over 7,000,000 tourists in its first five years, and contributing over £700m to the depressed economy of the region that was badly in need of a lift.

Additions since it opened include an education center, called the Core, which helps scientists, schoolchildren, and anyone with even a passing interest in gardening, to understand more about the diversity and importance of plants to our planet. Plans are in motion for a fourth Biome known as "the Edge," which will reproduce the arid and semi-arid regions of the world, and give a timely lesson on the true value of water and the dangers of climate change.

Visit the big blue caldera

When a volcano erupts with enough force, a caldera, or pit, is formed; and one of the biggest and most beautiful on the planet is Crater Lake in the remote wilderness of Oregon.

Calderas are the visible aftermath of volcanic activity—the super volcanos of disaster movies. They are formed when the force of the eruption is so great that the volcano literally implodes.

While its formation around 7,000 years ago must have been incredibly violent, Crater Lake is one of the most tranquil spots you can imagine. It is surrounded by the 180,000-acre Crater Lake National Park. The nearest airport is over an hour's drive away at Klamath Falls. The lake itself—the deepest in the USA—is six miles (10km) wide, and fringed by sheer cliffs capped with snow for most of the year. Most striking of all is the color of the water, an intense blue that looks as if it's been dyed. In fact, this striking hue is a result of its purity and depth.

Visit in the summer, since the park gets a tremendous amount of snowfall from October to April. While the water looks unbelievably tempting on a hot summer's day, the only safe swimming point is at the end of Cleetwood Cove Trail, which brings you right up to the water's edge.

OZ'S TURQUOISE VOLCANO

Blue Lake at Mount Gambier, Southern Australia, draws similar awe-struck reactions from visitors. However, while Crater Lake is pure blue, this caldera is filled with water of the most vibrant turquoise from December to February. No one knows for sure why it takes on such a Mediterranean hue, but it may be caused as calcium carbonate crystallizes in the searing summer heat.

Visit a town built on diamonds

Kimberley is a South African town that grew on the back of diamonds and even if it had wanted to forget its mining history, "the Big Hole" is there as a blood, sweat, and tears reminder.

Kimberley, in the Northern Cape, was once one of the richest places on earth—and all because of the discovery of chunks of carbon. Diamonds were discovered at Colesberg Koppie in 1871, and within a matter of years, Kimberley had grown into one of the most important commercial centers in South Africa and secured the sparkling future of De Beers.

Over 30,000 men were employed to hand-dig this seam of diamonds—and they kept on digging until they had created a giant pit 85ft (240m) deep with a perimeter of a mile. That patch of ground yielded around 15 million carats of diamonds until it was exhausted, eventually closing in 1914.

Visit and there is still no escaping "the Big Hole"; it is vast, although these days you can't see the bottom because of ground water. A museum with reconstructed buildings gives a flavor of Kimberley's past, and you can also see the Eureka, the first diamond discovered in South Africa.

MORE MIGHTY MANMADE HOLES

Mirna Diamond Mine Located in the permafrost of Eastern Siberia, this site is almost 2,000ft (610m) deep—so cavernous that flying over Mirna has been banned because of the dangerous air currents it generates.

Kennecott Utah Copper Mine Bingham Canyon, Utah This mine is the largest man-made excavation on earth, currently over two miles (3.2km) wide and 4,000ft (1,207m) deep. You can view this mighty hole at the site's visitor center.

Ogle the world's greatest diamonds

Want to locate a diamond as big as the Ritz? Well maybe not, but here are five choice gemstones in public collections that you can view from a safe distance through armor-plated glass.

1. Dresden Green

This diamond got its unusual hue because of exposure to radiation during its formation. Although small (41 carats) compared to most diamonds in public collections, its rarity makes it extremely valuable. It sits in the state art collection Grünes Gewölbe (Green Vault) in Dresden, Germany.

2. Hope

Reputed to be unlucky (perhaps it should have been called Abandon Hope), this beautiful, deep blue diamond was found in the early 1600s and had a checkered history until jeweler Harry Winston donated it to the Smithsonian Institute in Washington DC. It weighs in at almost 46 carats, and is displayed in the museum's hall of geology, gems, and minerals.

3. Koh-i-Noor

Once owned by Babur, the founder of the Mogul Empire, this priceless and enormous gem was presented to Queen Victoria in 1850. Later set into Queen Elizabeth, the Queen Mother's crown, it now resides in the Tower of London alongside other magnificent gems, including the 530-carat Cullinan I (also known as the Great Star of Africa).

4. Orlov

The origins of this half-egg shaped diamond are steeped in mystery, but it seems likely it may have formed the eye of a temple deity in Mysore, India, before eventually passing to the Russian royal family. It weighs almost 190 carats, and is a highlight of the Kremlin's Diamond Treasury.

5. Sancy

An unusual, pale yellow color, this stone has had several no- so-careful owners, including Henry III of France, Charles I of England, Prince Anatole Demidoff of Russia, and Lady Astor. It is now safely under lock and key at the Louvre in Paris.

Visit an ancient goldmine

The Romans didn't invade Britain for the weather, but because they recognized it as a lucrative source of minerals and precious metals. One of their prize finds was in the hills around Carmarthenshire, in Wales.

Dolaucothi Gold Mine in Pumsaint, Carmarthenshire is the only known Roman gold workings in the British Isles. This is a rich seam for archeologists today, with evidence of a fort and a settlement in this densely wooded river valley. The site was mined for around 60 years during the first and second centuries and you can see spoil heaps, channels, shafts, and the footings of buildings. The greatest archeological find was the remains of a water-lifting wheel—a rare piece of evidence of the sophisticated technology employed by the Romans.

Some historians believe the site may pre-date 100 AD, putting it on a par with ancient French mines. Although its existence was part of local lore—and it was even mined again from the 19th century until 1938—it was only identified as being an important Roman site in the 1960s. The area is now managed by the National Trust, and you can don a hard hat to visit underground workings.

While the seam of gold is no longer viable commercially, there is an opportunity to try panning for gold.

MINING BRITAIN

The Romans weren't just after British gold, but established mines for metal ore, copper, and tin. More vital still was lead, and mines in the Mendips, south of Bristol became the largest supplier to the Roman Empire of lead and its extract silver. Some caves here contain Roman artefacts, as well as objects dating back as far as the Mesolithic period.

Go panning for gold

There's gold in them thar hills—from Scotland all the way to Australia. Here are six places around the globe where, with a lot of patience, and a bit of skill, prospectors might just get lucky.

1. Jimtown 1849 Gold Mining Camp

Relive the heady prospecting days of the California 49ers by stopping off at this recreated gold-panning camp on the banks of Wood's Creek at Jamestown, California. Period costumes and grizzly gold rush characters are on the site, and you can learn how to pan and then keep any gold you find.

2. Lowther Hills

Scotland has quite a few seams of gold, but one of the best hunting grounds is around Wanlockhead and Leadhills in Dumfries and Galloway. This area once supplied gold for the Scottish royal family. Unfortunately, anything you find today officially belongs to the British Crown.

3. Pilgrim's Rest

South Africa's famous gold mining village in Mpumalanga (on the Panorama Route) has a dedicated visitor attraction called Diggings, where you can see how the earth was moved during the 19th-century gold rush. You can watch gold-panning demonstrations and try it yourself.

4. Pine Creek

This historical gold town in the Northern Territories, Australia, about two hours' drive south of Darwin, has lots of historical buildings to remind you of its rich past. Gold was discovered in 1870 by telegraph line workers, and you can go on organized panning trips (known here as gold fossicking).

5. Zlotoryja

This medieval gold and copper mining town in southwestern Poland has a museum dedicated to gold mining. The country's Guild of Gold Prospectors hosts the national gold-panning championships every year, during a heritage celebration known as Golden Week.

Go white-water rafting along the Amazon

Peru boasts some of the best white-water rafting in the world. Not only can you experience the thrills and spills of the rapids, but the journey takes you through vast canyons that lead from the snow-capped Andes to the lush Amazon.

A combination of fast rivers and awesome canyons makes Peru one of the world's top destinations for river adventures, whether you're a novice or a hardened river runner. The starting point for most beginner adventurers is Arequipa—also a great base for exploring the mighty Colca Canyon. The most popular short trip along Apurimac River takes you through a 985ft (300m) canyon, and includes plenty of fun rapids for novices, along with a few more fearsome falls. For adventurers, part of the magic of this journey is the majestic scenery, sandy beaches, and great wildlife viewing opportunities.

For a true wilderness trail, try a longer journey down Rio Tambopata. Here you mix wild water with periods spent floating silently along the Amazon headwaters, miles from civilization and surrounded by fabulous scenery in a national reserve.

THE ULTIMATE RAFTING CHALLENGE

Rio Cotahuasi is 11,490ft (3,500m) deep in places—by far the deepest canyon on earth. It starts its descent at the peak of Cerro Supramarca. It was only discovered by the rafting community in the early 1990s and has since become one of the ultimate challenges. Just getting into the water involves a grueling drive and hike. The reward includes plenty of Class IV and V rapids (that translates as very scary), plus amazing untouched pre-Inca ruins along the way.

Visit the world's most magnificent waterfalls

From Angel Falls in tropical Venezuela, to the glacier-fed spectacles of Norway and New Zealand, here are six of the most awesome sights on the planet.

1. Angel Falls, Venezuela

Not only is this the highest waterfall in the world at 3,200ft (979m), but its remote location makes it an adventure getting here. Most visitors take a flight from Caracas to Canaima, the national park surrounding the falls. The location was first spotted by American aviator James Crawford Angel— hence the name—although the original local name Kerepakupay Vena translates as Devil's Mouth.

2. Iguazu Falls, Argentina/Brazil

The sheer number of waterfalls is what draws visitors. There are over 270 in total spanning a two-mile (3.2km) stretch of the Iguazu River. Most are not that deep, typically 210ft (64m), but the almighty noise and turbulent water are breathtaking. You can access Iguazu from either country, although most of the falls are in Argentine territory. The best view of all is over Garganta del Diablo (Devil's Throat), a "U"-shaped cliff on the border.

3. Langfoss, Norway

Purists call this a cascade because it runs down the rocks rather than plunging in a sheer curtain, but you can't deny its drama as it spills down a 2,005ft (612m) mountain slope into the Åkra Fjord below. It never gets over-run with tourists, although there is a visitor area across the road from the fjord. Go in the summer when the mountain is lush and green.

4. Sutherland Falls, New Zealand

A stepped waterfall in Fjordland National Park on South Island, Sutherland Falls is famous partly due to its size, but also because it lies off Milford Track, the country's favorite hiking trail. The falls are fed by glaciers and Lake Quill, and then drop in three tiers to the Arthur River. It's one of a number of waterfalls along the track.

5. Tugela, South Africa

This waterfall in the Royal Natal National Park, around an hour's drive from Ladysmith, has five major tiers, and is part of a spectacular rock wall called the Amphitheater. You can hike to the top with the help of chain ladders, or view its 3,110ft (948m) drop from the Tugela Gorge at the bottom. Sometimes the top of the fall freezes in winter, creating huge columns of ice. The area is popular with hikers and also hosts the grueling mountaintop steeplechase known as the Mont-aux-Sources challenge.

6.Victoria Falls, Zambia/Zimbabwe

Also known as Mosi-oa-Tunya, this has to be one of the most photogenic waterfalls on the planet. Victoria Falls is fed by the Zambezi River, and forms a spectacular curtain as it tumbles down a chasm. It's the width of the falls that is most impressive as it spans almost one mile (1.7km) across, and in the rainy season 19 million cubic feet (500 million liters) of water tumble over the top every minute. Victoria Falls is a spectacle at any time of year, but the period from May to August usually offers the best photo opportunities.

Ride under a torrent

It's not the tallest—not even in the top ten—but Niagara is certainly the most visited waterfall on the planet. There are lots of great vantage points and ways to get very wet.

Famous as a honeymoon destination and a film location, Niagara Falls is also a popular side trip on any journey to Toronto or New York State. It has been a tourist hotspot since the 19th century, and these days around 20 million tourists visit each year—so don't expect to enjoy the splendor in isolation. Choice views from the Canadian side include a panorama from the top of the Skylon Tower and photo opportunities from Victoria Park. Or try the viewing deck on the US side in Prospect Point Park.

If you prefer to get a little closer—and don't mind heights—buy a ride on Whirlpool Aero Car, a cable car that has been operating since 1916, and takes passengers the 1,800ft (550m) over the Niagara River, giving clear views of the whirlpool below.

Closer still is the Journey Behind the Falls attraction, which takes you below Horseshoe Falls, the most spectacular of Niagara's three drops. Visitors used to be issued with sou'westers and rubber boots, but these days a biodegradable poncho provides protection against the spray. Most atmospheric of all is a journey through the bottom of the falls on the *Maid of the Mist*, a boat journey that has been run since the 1840s (although the boats have been updated). This is the best way to get the measure of Niagara's power as you journey past American and Bridal Veil Falls before being drenched by spray at Horseshoe Falls.

Find Europe's most picturesque waterfalls

Europe may not be in the super-league when it comes to thundering torrents of water, but it does offer waterfalls in spectacularly beautiful and remote settings. Here are five of the best.

1. Dettifoss

What it lacks in height it makes up for in water, since this Icelandic waterfall is reputed to be the most powerful in Europe. Fed by a glacial river, it tumbles into a canyon, and is at its most impressive after the ice melt. It is one of several waterfalls in Jökulsárgljúfur, a national park famous for its huge canyon.

2. Grande Cascade de Gavarnie

The highest in France at 1,385ft (422m), this tiered waterfall in the Hautes-Pyrénées tumbles into a spectacularly beautiful glacial amphitheater. It's a 30-minute trek from the nearest village, but worth the effort.

3. Krimmler Waterfall

Located in the far west of Hohe Tauern National Park near the Austrian city of Salzburg, this waterfall gushes down the Alps through thickly wooded countryside in three tiers from a height of 1,250ft (380m). You can follow a marked trail up the falls.

4. Staubbachfall

Staubbach is centerpiece of the picture-postcard village of Lauterbrunnen, Switzerland. It is one of several falls in the area, but is unique for its almost vertical drop down the cliff-face. The most idyllic viewing point is from a private balcony at Hotel Staubbach.

5. Steall Waterfall

This 395ft (120m) waterfall in Scotland drops over the side of the Nevis Gorge and is popular with visitors—not least because of the wobbly wire suspension bridge over the water, and the uplifting views to the Mamores Munros (mountains).

See the earth's power at work

Here are more locations keen vulcanologists should visit. They range from extremely active to extinct volcanos, but all are in stunningly beautiful locations, and give a glimpse of the earth's raw power.

1. Edinburgh, Scotland

It's a long time since this one smoked, but Scotland's capital is dominated by a volcano, and you can clearly see the effect of lava flows and vents that once shaped the landscape if you climb to the top of Arthur's Seat or Castle Rock. The site was probably active around 350 million years ago, but is still being pored over by geologists today.

2. Etna, Sicily

Europe's largest active volcano currently stands around 10,800ft (3,300m) high, and is perpetually bubbling away, although thankfully for local residents who benefit from the fertile soil on its lava fed-slopes, it is not considered among the highest risk volcanos. Nevertheless, it can still put on a huge show—footage of its 2002 eruption was used to represent Mustafar in *Star Wars Episode III: Revenge of the Sith*.

3. Nyiragongo, Democratic Republic of Congo

Although this volcano is off the standard tourist trail because of its remote location and ongoing unrest in the country, it is considered to be the biggest, and is certainly among the most dangerous in the world. The main crater is 820ft (250m) deep, and periodically contains a huge lava lake that threatens to spill down the mountain side.

4. Santorini, Greece

This group of volcanic islands in the Cyclades was the site of a huge eruption around 1500BC. These days it is famous for its amazing black beaches, and almost lunar landscape, and people like to get married overlooking the caldera. Scientists continue to monitor the islands closely for signs of volcanic life.

5. Teide, Tenerife

The third tallest volcano in the world, Pico de Teide on the Canary Island of Tenerife is a popular day-trip destination for tourists and naturalists, because it offers stunning views, and unique flora and fauna in the foothills. You need a special permit to climb all the way to the very top, but a cable car runs most of the way up. The last eruption was on the northwest flank in 1909.

6. Vesuvius, Italy

Clearly visible from Naples just across the bay, Vesuvius is a slumbering giant. The eerie lava-encased population at Pompeii is a salutary reminder of just how quickly it can wreak destruction. An eruption in 1944 destroyed three villages.

SKI DOWN A VOLCANO

New Zealanders head to Mount Ruapehu on the North Island because of its location in prime ski country, but it is also a highly active stratovolcano that last erupted in 1996. Risks to tourists in the region include "lahars"—volcanic mudflows that travel at speeds of up to 55 miles an hour (90km/h). Early detection cameras and warning systems are in place around the mountain, but this natural threat has not dampened the enthusiasm of hikers, skiers, and snowboarders. (For more on Mount Ruapehu, see page 209.)

Cruise one of the world's great rivers

Crossing countries, or continents, the world's great rivers offer wildlife, scenery, and a fascinating insight into the cultures you meet along the way. Here are four of the most exhilarating trips you can take.

1. Danube

Flowing from the Black Forest region of Germany to the Black Sea, this great waterway takes in some of the great cities and landscapes in Europe on a journey of more than 1,700 miles (2,735km). It may not always be as blue as the Strauss waltz implied, but its beauty is unquestionable, particularly if you cruise the stretch from Vienna to Budapest.

2. Mississippi

This river splices through the heart of the US. It begins at Lake Itasca, Minnesota, and travels down through eight states before flowing into the Gulf of Mexico. Along the way it's fed by numerous tributaries and remains one of the world's great commercial waterways. The most atmospheric cruises are on old-time steamboats such as the *Delta Queen*.

3. Nile

The longest river on the planet, this begins as two rivers in Ethiopia and Rwanda, converges in Sudan, and then flows north all the way to the Mediterranean. Head to Egypt, where the Nile has carved out the country's destiny, to see it at its most spectacular. There are endless cruise options, but the most popular route is from Luxor to the Aswan Dam.

4. Yangtze

Beginning in Tibet and flowing west to Shanghai, this is Asia's greatest river, and the third longest in the world. It passes through spectacular scenery. River cruises offer a leisurely and scenic way to cover major sites such as the Terracotta Warriors at Xian, and the mausoleum at Nanjing, as well as the mighty (and somewhat controversial) Three Gorges Dam.

Visit the world's deepest freshwater lake

Lake Baikal holds over a fifth of the world's surface water, and is also the oldest and deepest lake. Its isolation has allowed unique fauna and flora to thrive, earning it World Heritage site status.

Formed as a result of immense tectonic activity, Lake Baikal is estimated to be 5,370ft (1,637m) deep, but if you include the sediment below the water, the fissure in the earth's surface is a mighty five miles (8km) deep. Only when the Trans-Siberian Express reached this corner of southern Siberia was the extent of the lake first mapped (for the railway see page 125).

Its biodiversity is amazing, with over 1,000 plant species and 1,500 animal varieties. Over half are only found in this region, which is why it is of such importance. For visitors, one of the most enchanting spectacles is the lake's only mammal, the Baikal seal. This earless variety spends its whole life in freshwater and can live for over 55 years. No one knows exactly how it arrived so far from the sea, but scientists speculate that a corridor once linked the lake to the Arctic Ocean.

The tranquil blue water stretches over 1,300 miles (1,600km), so there is plenty to see. You can tour the periphery by rail (a ten-hour journey including 200 bridges), or join winter treks across it by jeep and dogsled. Truly adventurous souls can sign up for a Baikal Explorers' winter diving expedition. The water is pristine but chipping through the ice and swimming in temperatures averaging less than 39° fahrenheit (4° celsius) makes this a bracing experience.

See other great lakes

From North America's Great Lakes to the romantic and remote Caspian Sea, here are four inland waters that offer a combination of stunning scenery, fascinating wildlife, and hidden depths.

1. Caspian Sea

Covering an area of over 143,000 square miles (230,000sq km), this saline lake—biggest in the world by surface area—is bordered by Russia, Turkmenistan, Kazakhstan, and Iran, and its most famous product is the caviar-producing sturgeon fish. The easiest lakeside destination to get to is Kazakhstan's capital Baku.

2. Lake Eyre

Australia's great lake is in South Australia, and you may visit and find it dry, but the salt-pan basin around it is an essential part of this vast ecosystem. The lake has been full to capacity only three times in the past 150 years. Flooding occurs after seasonal rainfall, and then this arid landscape explodes with lush greenery, attracting huge numbers of pelicans, terns, avocets, and stilts.

3. Lake Superior

The largest of the Great Lakes and also the largest freshwater lake in the world by surface area, Superior is bounded by Ontario in Canada, and Minnesota, Wisconsin, and Michigan in the US. It is fed by 200 rivers and fringed by wilderness country. One of the most popular hiking routes is Superior Hiking Trail along the Minnesota shoreline.

4. Lake Victoria

With an area of some 26,000 square miles (41,8500sq km), Lake Victoria feeds the White Nile as well as bordering on Tanzania, Uganda, and Kenya. Many of its 3,000 islands are inhabited, and popular tourist destinations include Ssese Islands in Uganda. The entire shoreline offers great wildlife-watching opportunities; the best time to visit is during August and September.

Dive in a blue hole

Blue holes are amazing ocean formations that were created during the ice age as caves, and when the waters rose they filled up. One of the finest examples is the Great Blue Hole off the coast of Belize.

Made famous by Jacques Cousteau and now the site of countless diving and snorkeling tours, The Great Blue Hole lies around 60 miles (95km) from the mainland of Belize in the center of Lighthouse Reef. Surrounded by the turquoise waters of the Caribbean, this is a rich blue area measuring 300ft (91m). It looks almost perfectly circular and is around 480ft (145m) deep. While the waters inside the hole are not particularly rich in sea life, the limestone formations and huge stalactites that cling to its walls from about 100ft (30m) down are a remarkable sight.

Around the hole is a reef rich in shrimp and anemone along with angel fish, butterfly fish, and grouper. Bull sharks often patrol the perimeter, so divers and snorkelers tend to stick close to their buddies. The best way to get to the Great Blue Hole is on an organized boat trip from the mainland or from Caye Caulker.

BLUE HOLE ON THE BEACH

Officially the world's deepest, Dean's Blue Hole on Long Island, Bahamas is actually a vivid marine green. It sits in a picturesque bay surrounded by high cliffs, and is easily accessible by car from the capital Clarence Town or Stella Maris. The hole is right on the beach, and you only have to swim a few strokes to be suspended more than 665ft (200m) above the ocean floor.

Chill out in a crystal clear lagoon

The Blue Lagoon is such a vibrant shade of aquamarine that it looks like it has been tinted especially for a tourist brochure. Its location, off the north-west coast of Comino, Malta, provides shelter from the currents, and safe bathing in warm water.

Comino is a tiny rocky island between Malta and Gozo that over history has been a hideout for pirates, a home for lepers, and a stronghold for the Maltese military. With only a single hotel, most visitors to the Blue Lagoon arrive by ferry from one of the neighboring islands. It's worth the journey because it offers the most perfect swimming and snorkeling in calm and crystal-clear waters.

The lagoon is a sheltered bay between Comino and the tiny island of Cominetto, and its clear, sandy floor gives it a transparent quality—rare in this part of the world where deep waters and strong currents prevail. The best time to get there is early in the day, since tour boats and divers tend to congregate later on. Its photogenic qualities have been recognized by the film industry, and the lagoon has featured in *Swept Away,* and the American mini-series *Helen of Troy.*

TAKE A TRIP TO THE INLAND SEA

Dwejra on the Maltese island of Gozo boasts another calm lagoon known as the Inland Sea. It was created when two limestone caves collapsed, and is connected to the Mediterranean by a narrow tunnel. It has calm waters for swimming and snorkeling, and you can take a boat through to open water to see unusual rock formations along the coast, including Fungus Rock and Azure Window.

Watch nature let off steam

Old Faithful has been entertaining visitors to Yellowstone for generations, and the most miraculous thing about it is that it runs almost like clockwork—so it's almost certain to put in an appearance while you're there.

While hot springs occur across the planet in areas of geothermal activity, geysers are much rarer. They work a bit like an old-fashioned steam engine, except that it's a layer of molten rock deep underground rather than coal that provides the heat source. The water is super-heated, then rises up to ground level through a narrow fissure in the rock. There it explodes into the air in a cloud.

About half the geysers we know about are located in Yellowstone Park, and for many visitors, viewing Old Faithful is the highlight of the trip. It's not the tallest (that honor goes to Steamboat Geyser), but it is the most punctual, putting in an appearance around every 90 minutes. It's worth sticking around because when it does erupt, it sends a plume of boiling water up to 185ft (55m) into the air. Each spectacular show lasts anywhere from one to five minutes.

THE ORIGINAL GEYSER

Geyser is an Icelandic word and it comes from the Great Geysir, a spectacular 200ft (60m) spout that sadly hasn't been seen for decades. However, nearby Strokkur (this translates as "the Churn") usually appears every five minutes, setting off a jet of steam up to 100ft (30m) high. Both are located in Geysir thermal park in the south-west of the country, an otherworldly landscape where puffs of steam rise all around you.

Head to the world's best natural spa

At Iceland's Blue Lagoon you can bathe in algae and mineral-rich water heated to a perfect temperature, enjoy an invigorating shower under a waterfall, and then hunker down in a lava cave for a steam bath.

Spas don't get more back-to-nature than Iceland's Blue Lagoon. Just 45 minutes' drive from Reykjavik Airport, it offers a world-class pampering courtesy of the volcanos that much of Iceland is built on. This pool is filled with warm geothermal water tapped from a 6,000ft (2,000m) source deep underground. It is a year-round experience, but probably most scintillating during the snow, when locals and tourists alike shrug off their gray winter clothes, and revel in the heat and steam.

You can float on an air mattress in the middle of the lagoon, and be coated in silica mud and essential oils, or scrubbed with salt or algae (special blankets are provided to keep you warm). There's a sauna overlooking the lagoon and a steam bath carved out of a lava cave.

TWO MORE HOT SPOTS

1. ROTORUA, NEW ZEALAND
You can not only watch the bubbling volcanic mud that made this town famous, but check into Polynesian Spa. This historical site is on top of Priest Spring and has has been a bath house since the 1880s.

2. ATAMI, JAPAN
This coastal town is accessible from Tokyo and is one of the best places to experience "onsen," the hot spring baths that are a national institution. There are several in the town, which has been a resort for at least ten centuries.

CHAPTER 2

Animal Kingdom

 You can choose from a whole host of thrilling animal encounters—whether your taste runs to sunbathing with penguins, or swimming with sharks. We've included adventure trails on sea and land, as well as locations that get you close to the rarest animals on the planet.

There are also unique marvels of the living kindom, ranging from microscopic phosphorescent plankton, to the spectacular and truly prehistoric Komodo dragon.

See a living dragon

It's the world's largest species of lizard, but the Komodo dragon fits the bill for looks and fearsomeness, and has been known to kill humans. It is native to Rincah, Komodo, and neighboring Indonesian islands.

Full-grown lizards can grow to 10ft (3m) in length and they weigh around 155lb (70kg). Scarier still, they may eat up to 80 percent of their own body weight in one sitting. Despite their bulk, they charge prey, using their long, serrated teeth to inflict vicious wounds. The bite is bad, and the septicemia that generally occurs afterward is worse. The dragon's teeth harbor virulent bacteria, aided by its habit of biting its own gums when it eats, giving it blood-red saliva. It has a keen sense of smell, tracking dead or wounded prey to finish off at leisure.

There are estimated to be around 5,000 dragons in the wild, making this a vulnerable species. Reproduction isn't an easy affair as females bite and scratch at the first courtship approach. Eggs take seven months to hatch, and surviving hatchlings spend their early lives in trees to avoid becoming dinner for mom or dad.

There have been two recorded instances of females reproducing in zoos without a male participant. Scientists have suggested that this ability to conceive immaculately (known as parthenogenesis) would have been handy in the distant past—giving single female Komodo dragons an ability to colonize remote islands and establish a new population.

Your best chance of seeing a wild dragon is on an escorted tour from the island of Flores in the south-east of the Indonesian archipelago. Zoos with good populations include the Smithsonian in Washington DC.

Come face-to-face with a unicorn

The mythical beast that crops up so often in heraldry and medieval literature may have its origins in a real animal. Some historians have speculated that you can even encounter one today.

Unicorns appear in folklore and images around the globe—from India and the steppes of Russia, to Norway and Japan. You can see them on the Scottish coat-of-arms and view wonderful tapestries depicting the one-horned beast at Musée de Cluny in Paris, and the Metropolitan Museum in New York.

A skeleton of a unicorn was supposedly uncovered in the Harz Mountains of Germany in the 17th century—although nothing remains of it. Some have speculated that the unicorn was actually a rhinoceros, since this is the only mammal with one horn, but it is too ungainly and ill-tempered to convincingly fit the legend.

So for romantics, the most likely candidate for a living unicorn is the eland of southern Africa. It has the requisite grace and agility, and is capable of defending itself against a lion. It is considered to have spiritual and mythological properties by Africans, and is the animal most often depicted in east African rock art. Perhaps most convincing of all for would-be unicorn spotters is that, although it generally has two horns, some are recorded as being born with only one.

You will find the eland on the savannas and plains of southern and eastern Africa. Wildlife reserves in South Africa and Zambia's Zambezi National Park are the best places to spot them.

Encounter the world's rarest mammal

The northern white rhino is so endangered that it's believed there may only be four left in the wild, making it a strong candidate for world's rarest mammal.

Once it roamed the grassland of sub-Saharan east and central Africa, but now the last remaining population is in Garamba National Park in the Democratic Republic of Congo. Habitat loss, poaching, and now war have decimated its population (estimated at around 500 in the 1970s). It is almost impossible to come close to this animal in its natural habitat, but you can see small populations at San Diego Animal Park, USA and Dvur Králové Zoo in the Czech Republic.

Its close relative, the southern white rhino, is on the other hand a great conservation success story. Considered extinct at the end of the 19th century, a small population was found in South Africa, and a combination of breeding programs and protected habitats has seen the country's population grow to an estimated 15,000.

MORE CONSERVATION SUCCESSESS

1. GOLDEN LION TAMARIN This beautiful primate is native to lowland forests in Brazil. Still endangered, its population has increased thanks to habitat conservation.

2. BLACK FOOTED FERRET Once thought extinct, this small carnivorous North American mammal has been the focus of determined conservation efforts, including reintroduction into prairie habitats.

3. AMERICAN BISON The prairie's population of 60 million was hunted to the point of extinction in the 19th century. Breeding programs have seen their numbers swell. Yellowstone is the place to see them, but keep your distance as they cause far more injuries in the park than bears.

Hear the most elusive bird

Jerdon's courser has to be one of the rarest birds on the planet. After eluding ornithologists for 80 years, it was finally spotted in 1986 in a remote corner of Andhra Pradesh, eastern India.

So little is known about this bird's habitat or behavior that it takes luck or determined sleuthing to track it down, and estimates suggest that there are 200 or fewer in existence today. It is nocturnal, so most likely to be heard at dawn or dusk, and it has a yellow bill and a distinctive orange patch around the throat. There is one recording of its song—made by a British conservation scientist on a field trip in 2001, who was lucky enough to spot it in flight, and hear its distinctive "kwik-koo" call. In a bid to protect the bird, this recording has not been released to the wider public.

Conservation work focuses on protecting its habitat of scrub forests in the Sri Lanka Malleswara Wildlife Sanctuary, Andhra Pradesh—a corner of the Pennar river valley threatened by irrigation schemes. In an innovative attempt to track the bird, noise boxes issued to park rangers mimic the courser's cry, the aim being to find out more about its habitat and determine the true numbers in the region.

TWO ELUSIVE EUROPEAN BIRDSONGS

1. BITTERN A unique foghorn "boom-boom" cry signals this member of the heron family only found on reedbeds and marshy areas around the UK and Europe.

2. NIGHTINGALE This bird probably never sang in Berkeley Square even when it was more commonplace. Its song is most likely to be heard in southern Europe, although it will travel as far as southern Britain in summer, over-wintering in the African savanna.

Watch a pride of lions

Lions are the most sociable of big cats and watching them in a group is endlessly entertaining—although you won't need reminding that nature is red in tooth and claw if you head to Masai Mara game reserve in south-western Kenya.

The king of the beasts is a fine sight—from a safe distance—and one of the best places to view them is at Masai Mara, a huge game reserve in Kenya's Great Rift Valley, close to the border with Tanzania. Big cats are here because their food source is plentiful, with huge herds of wildebeest arriving on their annual migration every summer. You will spot zebra (also on the lion diet), giraffe, gazelle, plus hippos, and crocs around the Mara river itself.

Leopards and cheetah are frequently sighted, but lions steal the show for most visitors. This is the location the BBC chose for filming *Big Cat Diary*, a soap-opera-style nature program, recording the life of the prides living in the reserve, so you are almost certain to see a family group—possibly even a TV star—on your travels.

Choose from luxury camps inside the reserve, or more cheaper options outside its boundaries (where game is almost as plentiful). One of the best places to stay for game-viewing in comfort is the original lodge Keekorok, built right in the path of the wildebeest migration. Animals are so plentiful around the lodge during peak season (July to October) that you don't even have to stray outside the grounds to eyeball the animals.

Go on the trail of a tiger

Kanha National Park is Shere Khan territory—a classic *Jungle Book* setting where you might just be lucky enough to spot the rare and solitary Bengal tiger. Even if he proves elusive, the bird and animal life is spectacular.

The remote Mandia district of Madhya Pradesh is home to one of the largest populations of Bengal tigers. Bamboo forests and meadows are rich in spotted deer, antelope, and the endangered swamp deer, plus hyena, bison, leopard, and at least 170 varieties of birds. The reserve offers elephant safaris—a safe if precarious perch for wildlife viewing.

There are several lodges and hotels close to the reserve, but one of the most atmospheric is Tiger Camp, a collection of six tents surrounding a waterhole on the southern end of the reserve, created by a naturalist, and designed to create minimal environmental impact on this beautiful stretch of wilderness. Viewing opportunities are good all year, although the resorts and the reserve shut down from May to November because of the monsoon.

SEE ITS SUMATRAN RELATIVE

You will be lucky to spot the Sumatran tiger, the small and critically endangered cousin of the Bengal tiger, but the hunt is guaranteed to be exciting. Most of the estimated population of 400 lives in Sumatran national parks such as Kerinci Seblat—a spectacularly beautiful highland game reserve that is also home to rhinos, elephants, gibbon, and clouded leopards.

Come face to face with a liger

This offspring created by a male lion and a female tiger is the biggest cat in the world, and carries distinctive stripes but no mane. While the animal came to attention after the film *Napoleon Dynamite*, ligers have been recorded as far back as the early 19th century.

You are highly unlikely to see ligers roaming the plains or the jungle (although there have been unconfirmed reports of this strange cross-breed throughout history), since lions and tigers have different habitats. This might be a good thing since their resulting offspring are simply huge, standing over 4ft (1.2m) tall at the shoulder and up to 12ft (3.6m) on their hind legs. They have no mane, but do have the distinctive ruff of the tiger species. They also have faint stripes, usually mixed in with spots. Most curious of al,l they have inherited the tiger's love of water (lions hate it) and are enthusiastic swimmers. They may also have the sociable instincts of the lion, although sometimes—like Greta Garbo—they want to be alone.

In the US several reserves and sanctuaries have examples. At T.I.G.E.R.S., in Myrtle Beach, California, there's a giant liger which was bred at the center. There is another at Sierra Safari Zoo in Reno. On the East Coast you can see ligers at Wild Animal Safari in Pine Mountain, Georgia.

A tigon is the same genetic combination, except that the father is a tiger and the mother a lion. It is much smaller than a liger—possibly because lions have growth-inhibiting genes carried through the female line. It usually has both spots and stripes, and looks tiger-like in its head shape and form. While they are

THE FANTASMAGORICAL ZEEDONK

There are several spellings and names for a cross between a zebra and a donkey (including zebradonk, zonkey, and deebra). Take your pick but the animal is sometimes found wild in South Africa where donkeys and zebras have been in close proximity. It usually has the buff-colored coat of a donkey on its body, but stripes appear on the legs—making it look as if it's wearing socks. Like mules, these hybrids are infertile. In the UK a zeedonk was bred at Colchester Zoo, Essex and is still one of its most popular exhibits. Another can be seen at Groombridge Place Gardens near Tunbridge Wells, Kent, sharing a field with a donkey.

extremely rare now, they were more common as zoo exhibits in the 19th and 20th centuries. In India, it was common to breed tigons, and one called Ranji was famously presented to London Zoo in the 1920s.

These days the practice of inter-breeding tigers and lions is frowned upon by the zoological and conservation establishments, so most specimens you see are likely to be the result of an accidental encounter. While male ligers and tigons are infertile, the females are not, so there have been cases of further hybridization, resulting in li-tigons (lion cross with tigon), ti-ligers and so on.

Find a pink dolphin

Like something from a children's picture book, these dolphins are a startling candy-pink color. There are two species and both are considered extremely rare.

The Amazon river dolphin, or boto, is a freshwater species that inhabits the Amazon and Orinoco basins. If you're lucky, you might spot them in Venezuela, Colombia, Bolivia, or Peru. Although this dolphin is famous for its unusual color, not all botos are pink—in fact, most of the candy-colored varieties are male adults, and naturalists believe their hue may be due to scarring caused by territorial disputes with other males. The sure-fire way to get up close to these creatures is to sign up for a volunteering project such as Projeto Boto, giving access to the remote Mamiraué Institute for Sustainable Development in Brazil. There you join field trips to monitor the local pink dolphin population.

> ## SWIMMING WITH THE PINK DOLPHINS
>
> At Underwater World, Singapore, you can see pink dolphins in a special pool, and even sign up for a short swim and training session with the mammals. These one-to-one encounters are closely supervised by marine mammal trainers.

The Indo-Pacific humpback dolphin is an even pinker specimen, but found only in the waters around China—where, confusingly, it is known as the Chinese White Dolphin. The dolphins are born black, fade to gray, and then eventually take on their rosy coat with adulthood. The construction of Chek Lap Kok Airport at Lantau Island, Hong Kong, first brought this dolphin to wider public attention since this destroyed part of the animal's natural habitat. Now Hong Kong Dolphinwatch organizes boat trips around the harbor, donating a proportion of profits to conservation.

Encounter rare red squirrels

Britain's native red squirrel, immortalized as *Squirrel Nutkin* in the Beatrix Potter children's story, has become increasingly hard to spot as its numbers—and habitat—dwindle alarmingly.

It is smaller, shier, and most certainly cuter than its brash North American cousin, the eastern gray squirrel. Whereas the gray may be spotted in any urban park or suburban garden raiding the bird feeders, the red (actually more of a chestnut brown) is a solitary animal that requires a quiet patch of broad-leaved woodland, and plenty of nuts, although it will also eat fungi, shoots, fruit, and the occasional bird's egg.

There are estimated to be fewer than 150,000 red squirrels left in Britain (as opposed to almost 3,000,000 grays). The best places to see them are in the north of Scotland around Aberdeenshire, and the north of England around Cumbria and Northumberland. In north Wales there's a significant population on the island of Anglesey.

In the south of England, your best squirrel-spotting location is the Isle of Wight, where an estimated population of 3,500 survives in woodland. The mammal is so cherished here that you see signs on busy roads warning you to reduce your speed because this is red squirrel country.

MUTANT BLACK SQUIRRELS

A genetic mutation of the gray squirrel, the black's inky coat is caused by an excess of melanin. You sometimes find them in North America and the UK population was introduced at Woburn Abbey, where it still exists today. The most notable colony outside the park is in the Hertfordshire garden town of Letchworth, where black squirrels inhabit Howard Park and adjacent Norton Common.

Watch seahorses in action

Resembling miniature hobby-horses, these beautiful sea creatures swim upright, and some have a chameleon-like ability to change color and blend in with their surroundings.

Seahorses are found in the shallows in both tropical and temperate waters, sucking up larvae and small crustaceans through their long snouts. With their bony armor-plating and ability to change color to fit in with their surroundings—either to avoid attack or to catch prey—they can be hard to spot, but tend to be found in the shallows. Often they lurk among vegetation close to reefs, using their long tails to anchor themselves in strong currents. Perhaps the most remarkable fact about seahorse biology is that it is males, not females, that give birth to the young known as fry. Most species are also monogamous, adding to their romantic appeal.

Around 35 species have been recorded, and some of your best viewing grounds are off the coast of Australia and Indonesia. Here you can find truly exotic specimens like *Hippocampus bargibanti* which can take on a rainbow of colors depending on its location. Although you might spot them out snorkeling, usually the best way to get up close is on an organized dive.

DRAGONS OF THE DEEP

The seahorse's close relative, the leafy seadragon, is an even rarer treat. It has strange plant-like appendages attached all along its body to provide effective camouflage. Seadragons can be found around the coast of southern and western Australia. One of the best places to go searching for them is off the jetty in Rapid Bay, which holds a biennial festival in their honor. You'll also find them around Waubs Bay and Waterfall Bay, Tasmania.

Go manatee watching

The manatee, or sea cow, is one of the gentle giants of the oceans, grazing on vegetation around shallow saltwater bays, estuaries, and coastal waters. One of the best places to spot them is in Florida.

With their long tails and gentle bovine faces, manatees are thought to be the source of the mermaid myth. Since they stick to the shallows and frequently come up for air, it seems likely they came into frequent contact with fishermen and sea voyagers.

While Amazonian manatees stick to river estuaries, their larger West Indian cousins (measuring around 10ft/3m long) migrate between warm waters in Florida in winter and the southern states along the Eastern Seabord in summer. Your best viewing areas are Blue Spring State Park between Orlando and Daytona Beach, and Lee County Manatee Park at Fort Myers. Populations also congregate around power stations because of the warm water they generate—try Tampa Electric Company's viewing center in Apollo Beach, where up to 300 animals gather from November to April.

SPOT A DUGONG

The manatee's close cousin is the dugong, found all around the Indo-Pacific, although the largest remaining population is off northern Australia. The animal grazes on sea grasses in sheltered areas, usually leaving a telltale trail of uprooted plants behind it. Dugong are shy and retiring animals, but you may be lucky enough to spot a family group. There's a good population around Moreton Bay near Brisbane, and if you aren't lucky enough to see one, other underwater wildlife treats include turtles, dolphins, and gray nurse sharks.

See a synchronized firefly show

In Kuala Selangor, Malaysia, you are guaranteed fireflies. Such is their profusion in this tropical region that you can watch them signaling to each other every night of the year in a spectacular courting ritual.

While fireflies—also known as lightning bugs—are a rare and seasonal sight in temperate regions, in more tropical climates they can be relied on night after night. Indeed, at Bukit Belimbing, around ten minutes' drive from the town of Kuala Selangor, they are so confident the fireflies will show up that they have created a small resort based around them.

The fireflies (actually a form of beetle) use light to attract a mate, and the Selangor River is a perfect habitat for them because of its mangrove trees, known locally as Berembang. The mating display usually begins an hour after sunset, and is at its peak for around three hours, although the flickering can be seen until dawn. The effect of so many fireflies signaling in sequence is otherworldly and the best way to view them is to take a nocturnal boat trip along the river. This is an especially popular location at Christmas when the fireflies act as natural fairy lights.

THE ELKMONT LIGHTNING BUGS

You need to drive up into the Great Smoky Mountains to see the USA's most famous firefly show. Like the lightning bugs of Malaysia, Elkmont's beetles put on a synchronized display, although the Tennessee variety perform for a much shorter season. Your best time to visit is mid-June, and the display usually starts at around 9.30pm around the nature trail close to the river. Access is via highway 441

Visit a magical illuminated cave

The fungus gnat may sound like something you'd squash or swat, but it is a thing of beauty. This star performer is responsible for a magical cave, which has become one of New Zealand's most popular visitor attractions.

Not many insects have been serenaded by Kiri Te Kanawa, but such is the fame of Waitomo Glow Worm Caves that the famous diva once sang an aria here. This North Island limestone cave complex is renowned for its Cathedral Cavern and magnificent stalactites and stalagmites, but it's the tiny *Arachnocampa luminosa* that inhabit the ceiling of Glow Worm Grotto that most people come to see.

Boat tours take visitors through the caves and into the grotto where thousands of larvae of the fungus gnat line the walls and ceiling. They emit an eerie, blue-green light which is strongest when they are hungry (it's how they attract the insects they feed on). They spend up to nine months glowing in the dark before emerging as adults. As the adult gnats have no mouth they can't feed—or bite—and once they have mated, they lay their eggs and die, leaving the next generation of larvae to continue the light show.

GO ON A GLOW WORM SAFARI

In the northern hemisphere glow worms light up the darkness from around mid-June to mid-July. They are from the same family of beetle as fireflies, but only the females do the glowing—climbing to a prominent point to lure a suitable mate. They are fond of slugs and snails, and tend to be most common in areas of chalk or limestone soil. Best hunting grounds are around canals and rivers, but they can sometimes be found on disused railroad banks and woodland edges.

Swim in a luminous bay

There is a hidden bay in the Spanish Virgin Islands, where, provided time and tides are right, you are guaranteed the most spectacular phosphorescent display.

This luminous light (technically it's known as bio-luminescence) makes water glow blue-green. It's an incredible sight, made all the more special because it's so hard to predict when and where it will happen—unless you head to Bahia Mosquito on the island of Vieques. The island is rich in flora and fauna, but light on tourists—most fly in from neighboring Puerto Rico to chill out in one of the last remaining wilderness spots in the Caribbean.

The bio-luminescent waters in Bahia Mosquito are caused by plankton called dinoflagellates. They measure around a twentieth of a millimeter, and emit a powerful light when they are disturbed. In this bay there are estimated to be almost 700,000 of them per cubic foot (that's 7,000,000 per cubic metre). Their existence in such vast numbers depends on a fragile set of environmental circumstances. The bay is surrounded by mangroves, which release a nutrient-rich cocktail into the water. It is also pollution-free and has a narrow channel to allow water to be refreshed, but keeps the temperature reasonably constant and protects organisms within the bay.

Whatever the science behind their presence here, for visitors it is pure magic, especially since on Island Adventures' boat trips around the bay (powered by electricity to avoid oil pollution) there is a chance to swim in the water and have the sensation of being surrounded by stardust. Trips should be timed around the moon— your best light show comes when the moon is least visible.

Watch a living laser show

The Australian giant cuttlefish is huge, growing up to 5ft (1.5m) in length. A strange enough spectacle, but during the mating season, these cephalopods congregate to put on a multicolored light show.

Giant cuttlefish (*Sepia apama*) are worth the price of a dive at any time of year because their balletic movements underwater are mesmerizing. They can shoot through the water, employing a form of jet propulsion (they do this by taking in and then expelling water), or tread water gracefully using their side fins.

Cuttlefish are naturally curious about divers and will swim up close and "eyeball" you—only expelling a harmless cloud of ink when they feel threatened. The best viewing time is from May to September when millions congregate around the south coast of Australia to find a mate. Then they use their ability to change color to dramatic effect.

Male cuttlefish have a battle of the light shows—using pigment sacs under their skin to create stripes of vivid purple, green, or blue. Sometimes a group will battle it out, each cuttlefish going through their rainbow repertoire until one of them emerges as the victor, and can turn his dazzling seduction technique on the awe-struck females. The male fertilizes eggs in a pouch under the female's mouth, and golfball-sized eggs are then deposited in crevices around the reef. After several months the hatchlings emerge, taking over two years to reach adulthood.

This attraction has put Whyalla, South Australia firmly on the tourist map and diving schools take parties out to the reef around Black Point and Point Lowly from an area known as Cuttlefish Boardwalk. Non-divers can also enjoy the show as snorkeling also gives views of the cuttlefish in action.

Go swimming with dolphins

These amazing and sociable sea mammals are a joy to watch in the water, and the chance to interact with them is one of the great sea adventures. Here's a selection of holiday locations where you may get lucky.

1. Azores

This group of Atlantic islands offers plenty of dolphin-watching opportunities, and up to eight species are regularly sighted, along with sperm whales. Escorted boat trips offer the chance to snorkel close to their habitat.

2. Bahamas

The shallow and clear waters around Bimini are famous for their population of Atlantic spotted dolphins. The animals are used to seeing humans in the water, and boat tours give you the chance to watch their underwater gymnastics.

3. Egypt

Red Sea coral reefs are home to spinner dolphins, and this sheltered bay is suitable for snorkeling as well as diving. There's also the chance of seeing rays, turtles, or the rare dugong (see page 57).

4. Wales

Cardigan Bay is famous for its beauty and its resident bottlenosed dolphins, with an estimated population or around 120. You may also see harbor porpoise and gray seal. The harbour wall at New Quay is a good spot to get close to them.

THE BOTTLENOSED DOLPHIN HOTSPOT

Monkey Mia in Shark Bay, Western Australia has an extraordinary reputation for these creatures. Back in the 1960s a pod began swimming into the shallows to interact with humans. They now make several visits a day—usually in the morning. Visitors are allowed to assist with feeding the dolphins under the close supervision of rangers.

Try a close encounter with sharks

Diving with sharks is one of the ultimate thrills, but for a close encounter you will never forget, head to Shark Alley in South Africa to get up close to the mighty great whites.

The heavyweight of the shark world is the great white—up to 20ft (6m) in length, with fearsome jaws and an even more fearsome reputation. Its major predator is man and this vulnerable species is a rare sight in most waters. However, if you want to see sharks in abundance, head to Dyer Island, close to Cape Town, South Africa.

Local tour companies offer the chance to watch from the relative safety of the boat, or experience the ultimate *Jaws*-style encounter and get lowered into the water in a shark cage. The sharks are attracted by chum—an unsavory mixture of fish entrails and blood—and will come right up to the boats to feed. You are protected by the steel cage and sit alongside the boat below the water line. In most instances, sharks are only interested in the food being thrown in the water, although sometimes they will brush past the cage, close enough to touch. At this point a small voice in your head reminds you how much more substantial you look than the sardines on offer from the boat.

The peak cage-diving season lasts from April to September—later on in the year sharks have a plentiful supply of seal pups. While no cage-diving fatalities have been recorded yet, it is controversial, and has been banned in some waters (including Florida) because of concerns that it is making sharks associate humans with mealtimes.

Sunbathe with penguins

One of the most surreal wildlife viewing experiences is to lay your towel down on Boulders Beach, catch the sun's rays, and wait for the penguins to come and join you.

Around 20 minutes' drive from Cape Town you reach Simon's Town, a pretty village nestling in a quiet bay on the way to Cape Point. The main draw here are the jackass (also known as African or black-footed) penguins. These cute but noisy birds think this is their beach too, so it's usual to find yourself basking in the sun next to one. Although they are tame and unflustered by the presence of people, they can inflict a nasty nip if you invade their space or bother them.

The breeding population started as a pair in the 1980s, and has grown so dramatically that they have become something of a town nuisance—invading gardens and wrecking plants. A fence has discouraged this loutish behavior and Boulders Beach has become one of the major attractions of Table Mountain National Park.

PENGUINS ON PARADE

Phillip Island is an island around 85 miles (140km) south of Melbourne where you can watch the Penguin Parade, an event so magical it could almost have been choreographed by Disney. Every day at dusk, little penguins (also known as fairy penguins) make their way back to their burrows in the sand dunes after a hard day's fishing. Traveling in organized groups, they waddle across Summerland Beach watched by crowds of love-struck tourists. You can view the whole show from a boardwalk behind the beach.

Go whale watching

The most magnificent and awe-inspiring of sea mammals offers extraordinary diversity—from the majesty of the blue whale to the acrobatics of the humpback. Here are top whale-watching locations.

1. Grand Manan, Canada

This fishing island sits at the entrance to the beautiful Bay of Fundy in New Brunswick. Tours regularly spot the humpback and North Atlantic right whale. You may also see minke and finback whales. Try to take in Machias Seal Island for the sight of colonies of Atlantic puffin and razorbill auk.

2. Kaikoura, New Zealand

A former whaling town on South Island, this offers spectacular scenery and history. Huge sperm whales are year-round residents, but you may also see humpback, pilot, blue, and southern right whales. This is also a mecca for fur seals and albatross.

3. Mull, Scotland

The Gulf of Hebrides has warm waters that attract a variety of species during the early summer months including minke whales,

orcas, and basking sharks. You may be lucky and spot sei whales and northern bottlenosed dolphin.

4. Orcas Island, US

One of the San Juan Islands located about an hour's ferry ride from Anacortes, Washington State, this island has a large colony of resident orcas between mid-April and September. You can see them from the shore at Whale Watch Park, or take an organized boat or kayak ride. They are here for the salmon run, and you should also find seals, sea lions, and eagles in the vicinity looking for a gourmet meal.

5. Reykjavik, Iceland

Whales are almost guaranteed in Icelandic waters, and you can even take tours from the capital's harbor to see minke and humpback whales along with dolphin, porpoises, and a huge variety of seabirds.

Wrestle giant crabs

Norway's red king crabs are like creatures from the deep lagoon, measuring up to 6ft (1.8m) across, with fearsome spiky shells and bulbous eyes on stalks. They are also really tasty.

Their freakish proportions may look like something out of a sci-fi comic but they are the result of an innocent if misguided Soviet experiment. Scientists in the 1960s decided these natives of Kamchatka, in eastern Siberia, would be a good way of adding a little luxury to the diet of the population, so brought them over 2,000 miles (3,200km) to the Arctic for farming. A few escaped across the Barents Sea where the climate and lack of natural predators proved so favorable that they grew both in dimensions and in population. The first red king crab was spotted in northern Norway around a decade later.

Now there are millions of the boggle-eyed beasties and their march south (around 30 miles/48 km a year) means they are being closely monitored to assess their impact on the marine environment. Some speculate that they might end up in British waters within the next four decades, which could make fishing in rock pools a dangerous contact sport.

One benefit of their invasion of Norwegian waters is that they have become a valuable cash crop for fishermen. The giant claws make extremely good eating, although the body is unpalatable. Tourist fishing trips—usually combined with snowmobile treks and other winter sports—are run from Finnmark county, right at the top of Norway. The best time to catch a red land crab is between September and February. Just watch out for those claws.

Find great alien survivors

Take an animal out of its natural setting and give it a new home with no natural predators, and the results may not always be what you had hoped. Here are five that have thrived outside their native environment.

1. Camel
Imported to Australia to help open up the remote desert regions, the population is now up to a million. They can decimate the landscape during periods of drought. Enterprising Australians export them back to the Middle East.

2. Cane toad
Introduced to Queensland, Australia to control sugar-cane beetles, these puffed-up amphibians are rather too good at their job, killing snakes, birds, and even crocodiles.

3. Common brushtail possum
Brought to New Zealand to establish a fur industry. Now the population is estimated at 60,000,000 (15 times the human population), and the cute bushy-tailed critters are a menace to native trees and wildlife.

4. Parrot
Once a popular pet, escaped parrots have gone native in parts of London and the Home Counties. A recent research project suggested the population was growing at 30 percent a year and could be as high as 20,000. In the future this could have implications for both commercial fruit growers and native birds.

5. Tiger
Unlikely as it sounds, estimates put the US population of tigers at 10,000—double that found in the wild. Most are held in private zoos or owned as pets. They don't make loyal companions. In 2003 police removed a Bengal-Siberian tiger called Ming from a five-room New York apartment after it got into an altercation (which it won) with its animal-mad owner.

Meet Crocodile Dundee

No one actually wrestles the reptiles at Darwin Crocodile Farm, but you can see these monsters munching their lunch, view the world's largest white crocodile, and then sample a croc burger to remind the giant beasts who's boss.

A short drive south from Darwin along the Stuart Highway, this farm houses around 36,000 crocodiles—ranging from hatchlings to adult males up to 16ft (5m) from snout to tail. These are animals you wouldn't want to approach, but game-wardens venture inside the enclosures during feeding times to demonstrate to onlookers just how cavernous a croc's jaws can be.

Star of the show is Snowy, billed as the largest white crocodile in the world. But since the visitor area is full of waterholes and trees, you will find plenty of opportunities to watch the animals in their natural setting—basking in the shade or floating along the water.

Many of the crocs here are destined to become belts, bags, or burgers, but this is actually part of a conservation success story. Back in the 1950s the saltwater crocodiles that inhabited the Northern Territories were fair game for commercial hunters, and over the following two decades they were threatened with extinction. After state protection the population recovered and eventually farming licences were issued. Facilities such as Darwin Crocodile Farm maintain a breeding stock, and can supplement the wild population with its own hatchlings should the need arise.

Farming such a gigantic and fearsome beast requires a special kind of animal husbandry. Removing eggs from the nest is particularly risky—only the most experienced are enlisted for the chore. Matchmaking is also a skilled business, since male crocs have a habit of killing prospective mates before they've had the chance to be properly introduced. Aggressive males tend to be kept off the breeding program, and the farmers allow one waterhole per crocodile so they can maintain their own space.

FOUR MORE PLACES TO FIND CROCS AND ALLIGATORS

1. BHITARKANIKA MANGROVES
This important mangrove nature reserve in Orissa on the north-eastern coast of India is home to a population of around 700 endangered saltwater crocodiles, as well as the even rarer olive ridley sea turtle.

2. FLORIDA
The American crocodile is an endangered species (you can tell it from the much more common American alligator because its teeth are always visible). Best viewing grounds are around Biscayne and Everglades National Parks in Florida.

3. JOHANNESBURG
The Nile crocodile is almost as fearsome a maneater as Australia's saltwater crocodile. You can see them across sub-Saharan Africa, but safe viewing is guaranteed at Croc City Crocodile Farm at Gouteng, north of Johannesburg.

4. YANGTZE RIVER
Unlike its US cousin, the Chinese alligator is severely threatened, with its habitat along the lower Yangtze being disturbed by agriculture. It is smaller than the American alligator and may spend over half the year in hibernation.

Encounter the world's most dangerous animal

While travelers to exotic regions may live in fear of marine predators and crocodiles, without doubt it's the humble mosquito that causes the most problems by transmitting illnesses such as malaria.

Whether you know it as a mozzie, a skeeter, or a bug, it can be a real nuisance when it bites, and a killer in some areas of the globe. Only the female mosquito supplements a diet of nectar and fruit juice by feasting on human blood. The resulting itchy bumps are caused by our immune system's reaction to a cocktail of mosquito saliva and anti-coagulants injected under the skin through her serrated proboscis.

There are around 3,500 species—thought to have evolved during the Jurassic era 170,000,000 years ago when they were considerably larger. It's the anopheles mosquito that causes the major health problems, transmitting malaria, encephalitis, West Nile, and dengue fevers.

Mosquitos are most active at dawn and dusk, although malarial varieties can and do bite at any time of day. The best treatment is prevention. In communities this means minimizing breeding grounds (typically still water and marshy areas), and for individuals the answer is to cover up, use insect repellent, and mosquito nets. Travelers are also advized to take anti-malaria tablets. Affected regions include Central and parts of South America, most countries in sub-tropical Africa, and southern and eastern Asia.

While there is no clear evidence that some people are more prone to be bitten, there are plenty of anecdotes. In the British Armed Forces it used to be said that if mosquitos enjoyed feasting on you, leeches left you alone!

Find small but deadly beasties

Australia may have legendary sunshine and beaches, but it also has a world-class array of killer wildlife. Forget the sharks and the crocs, there are far more diminutive beasts out to get you.

1. Blue-ringed octopus
There are four species to watch out for, including one found around the Great Barrier Reef. The golf-ball-sized octopus will bite if touched or provoked, and carries enough venom to paralyze a victim and stop the heart. If it is glowing blue it's a sign to watch out.

2. Box jellyfish
Also known as the sea wasp, this bell-shaped creature's toxic tentacles can stop the heart in less than four minutes. It is common in north-eastern Australia, where warning signs are displayed around beaches and estuaries in the summer months.

3. Funnel-web spider
With a bite that can pierce a fingernail, the Sydney funnel-web (*Atrax robustus*) is feared because males—which, in this instance, are more deadly than females—tend to leave the burrow, and wander into houses or garages in search of a suitable mate.

4. Red back spider
A close relative of the black widow, this arachnid is distinguished by a red stripe down its back. Part of the problem is its small size—the deadly females measure less than 0.5in (1cm) long. It also has a habit of hanging out in urban areas, often setting up its web in dark corners of sheds and outhouses.

5. Stonefish
Effectively camouflaged by resembling a rock, this fish lives in shallow waters and feeds on small fish and shrimp. While not actively aggressive, the danger to humans comes when they step on it as the fish's back is armed with barbed dorsal spines that can kill in two hours without anti-venom.

Stalk the monarch of the glen

Landseer's famous portrait of the red deer is a romanticized image of this majestic beast. Even today it's not hard to find them roaming wild—and in parts of the Scottish Highlands they are considered a pest.

The UK and Ireland's largest deer *Cervus elaphus scoticus* is an imposing beast, standing over 4ft (1.35m) to the shoulder with antlers that can be about 3ft (1m) long. Their natural habitat is diverse: covering woods, moors, and grassland. You find isolated pockets of them in Wales, England, and Ireland, and without their natural predators, wolves and lynxes, they have become so common in Scotland that some conservationists and landowners consider them a pest. Another more damaging threat has come from interbreeding with non-native sitka deer, and it's thought that in time the last pure red deer in Scotland will be restricted to outlying islands such as Rum.

The best sighting spots are around Galloway Forest Park, Perthshire, and the north western Highlands. The deer tend to stick to the high ground in summer, and come down to the glens in winter in search of food. The most spectacular viewing time is during the fall rut in October, when stags lock horns in order to secure a coterie of females.

SEE RED DEER IN LONDON

Within a stone's throw of central London, Richmond Park has a population of around 300 red deer and an even larger herd of smaller fallow deer. This is a romantic setting with its ancient oaks, and you can get close enough for fabulous photo opportunities.

Spot a moose on the loose

An unforgettable sight with its forked antlers, long snout, and gangly legs, the moose (or elk) is such a common animal in parts of Canada, the US, and Scandinavia that it's a traffic hazard.

Head to New Brunswick in Canada, Alaska, or the northern states of New England and you can't miss the traffic signs, even if the moose proves elusive. The largest of all deer is an ungainly creature, less monarch of the glen than hazard of the road, due to its unfortunate habit of blundering into cars. Hitting any large animal is dangerous, but a moose can be lethal because its huge size and skinny legs means it can end up on—or sometimes in—the vehicle.

Despite its comical appearance, this is an animal supremely well adapted to its habitat. Its legs make it a powerful swimmer and a long neck enables it to pull tender shoots off high branches. Those thick lips are handy for stripping greenery off the most unpromising twig.

It is considered the national animal of Canada, Sweden, and Norway, and in Russia, elk milk is used to treat anemia and ulcers. If you want to see those fabulous antlers, go in summer or fall when the males shed them after the rutting season, and new ones don't grow until the following spring. For a guaranteed moose sighting, head to Russia's elk farm at a forest reserve outside Kostroma. It has a small domesticated herd and allows visitors to pet and feed them.

Watch the world's last wild horses in action

The Przewalski (or takh) are the last remaining truly wild horses on the planet, and in order to see these magnificent creatures you have to journey to the remote regions of Mongolia.

Unlike domestic horses, or even those we consider wild (see facing page), the Przewalski is a reminder of far-distant times when herds of these beautiful creatures roamed Europe and Asia. Long before it was domesticated, the horse was hunted for meat, as ancient cave paintings in France and Spain indicate. Even as recently as the 15th century, there were many wild herds in existence in Europe.

Today, this wild animal is among the most endangered species, with population estimates of fewer than 1,500. It was declared extinct from the wild in the 1960s but after captive breeding programs, herds have been reintroduced into Mongolia, where it is the national symbol. Standing around 12 hands high, it looks more like a well-built pony. The coat varies but is usually beige or dun with a lighter muzzle, and a dark mane and tail. It has a distinctive dark strip down its spine and stripes on the legs like a zebra. Most importantly, it has 66 chromosomes, compared to 64 in other horses.

The best place to see Przewalski in action is at Hustai National Park, about a two-hour drive from the Mongolian capital Ulaan Baatar. There are tourist camp sites and pony trekking trips available, and it's the historical hunting ground for former khans (kings) of Mongolia. Ancient temples and neolithic graves are dotted around this stepped landscape, and the shy, wild horses can be admired from a safe distance.

See horses and ponies running free

While Mongolia may be home to a truly wild species, there are other breeds of feral horses and ponies that still roam the land and enjoy special privileges. Here are four top spots to find them.

1. Assateague Island, USA

Chincoteague (or Assateague) ponies live on this island off the Eastern Seaboard. There are romantic theories about their origin involving a wrecked Spanish galleon, but it seems more likely they are descendants of early colonists' livestock. While ponies on the Maryland side are cared for by the US Park Service, the ones in Virginia belong to the local fire department.

2. Brecon Beacons, Wales

A semi-wild breed, Welsh mountain ponies date back at least 3,000 years. What they lack in stature they make up for in sturdiness, making them a popular choice for domestication (one that can stand up to novice child riders). You can still see a small wild population roaming the Black Mountain region of Brecon Beacons National Park.

3. Camargue, France

The windswept plains of southern France are home to one of the oldest and most celebrated varieties. Born black or brown, Camargue horses fade to pale gray or white at adulthood. They are strictly protected and managed to ensure purity of the bloodline in this remote and spectacularly beautiful national park.

4. New Forest, England

The English native breed of pony has inhabited this ancient Hampshire forest since at least 1016 and still runs free today—although with careful management. Typically chestnut (although almost any color is allowed) New Forest ponies graze alongside pigs and cattle, and help maintain the woodland setting.

Cuddle a koala

Visitors to New South Wales can admire but not hold koalas, so you'll need to journey north to Queensland to discover what it feels like to cuddle one of the cutest animals on the planet.

Although this is one of the symbols of Australia, koalas only inhabit the east of the country, and in many places, encroachment of humans has put their population under severe threat. The best place to see them is in a sanctuary—but since New South Wales banned cuddling them, your best bet is to visit Lone Pine Koala Sanctuary, near Brisbane.

Here the marsupials sit in trees for most of the time, chomping on eucalyptus leaves. Their dozy expression and seemingly endless capacity for sleep is not because they are drunk, it's just that eucalyptus is a very poor nutritional source, so they conserve their energy by snoozing for up to 19 hours a day.

At Lone Pine, the koalas are only allowed to be cuddled for 30 minutes a day with one in four days off to ensure they get enough time to eat and sleep, but with 130 of them "on the staff," there are still plenty of photo and film opportunities for visitors. Other animal interactions include kangaroo and wallaby feeding, and dingo patting.

WHERE TO SEE THEM IN THE WILD

Although you can't guarantee a wild koala sighting in urban Australia, you're almost certain to spot one on Kangaroo Island in South Australia. The species was introduced here, and has bred so prolifically that there have been frantic efforts to control the population. The island is also a top spot to see Tammar wallabies (also considered a pest) and Australian sea lions.

Meet a giant panda

It has become an emblem of the conservation movement, and an irresistible draw for zoo goers, but the giant panda is an elusive bear and your best chance of seeing it in the wild is in Qinling Mountain range.

With its trademark black patches and roly-poly physique, the panda is a star of the animal kingdom. Regaled with tales about its unwillingness to procreate, and images of it peacefully munching on bamboo behind zoo bars, it's easy to imagine this as a perpetual victim of progress. In fact, conservation progress is being made by the Chinese government.

The Qinling Mountain range in central China's Shaanxi Province is home to one of the largest populations of panda, and new reserves and wildlife "corridors" are helping to sustain the habitat of this reclusive bear, along with other rare animals such as the red panda and golden monkey. Organized tours allow you to explore this habitat in the company of expert guides.

It is one of 33 reserves established in China to sustain the panda. A ban on logging in Sichuan, Shaanxi, and Gansu provinces is also designed to protect its forest habitat. A breeding program at Wolong Nature Reserve, Sichuan, aims to return more pandas to the wild, and you can also visit this reserve—part of which is a UNESCO World Heritage site. Since the panda is a shy beast, it is notoriously difficult to accurately estimate the numbers remaining in the wild, but most figures put the population at around 1,600. However DNA analysis at one reserve has suggested there could be almost double that number—something that should please panda-lovers everywhere.

Watch a hummingbird feed

This iridescent bird may look delicate, but it is capable of flying vast distances on its annual migration. The best way to see one in action is to visit a North American garden.

Hummingbirds are one of the tiniest showstoppers on the planet. Weighing in at 0.1oz–0.7oz (anything from two to 20 grams), these amazing birds feed by hovering over a nectar source, their wings flapping so fast they appear as a blur. This hyper-activity can mean a heartrate of more than 1,200 beats a minute, so they require vast quantities of energy. This is why it is so common to see them sucking sugary nectar up through their long beaks.

There are over 300 species found throughout the Americas, from Alaska to southern Argentina, as well as the Caribbean. The most common variety in North America is the Ruby-Throated Hummingbird, which makes the long trek to Central or South America for the winter. There was a persistent myth that they rode piggyback on larger birds, but now it is recognized that these tiny birds are prodigious flyers—even crossing the Gulf of Mexico without a rest stop.

For North Americans, the hanging of the birdfeeders is a spring ritual. The feeders (usually red or orange to attract the birds) are filled with a sugar-and-water solution and, provided the location is right, the reward is to get up close to a hummingbird and watch it feed on a daily basis. Sometimes the same bird will return to its favorite feeder year after year.

See a host of bald eagles

America's national symbol is a magnificent bird to watch in flight, but your best sighting experience is at Alaska's Chilkat Bald Eagle Preserve where an annual gathering offers a spectacular photo opportunity.

The bald eagle has been a symbol in the US for centuries. To Native Americans, they were sacred and during the War of Independence they came to represent freedom. Although you see the bird's image on everything from coins to the Great Seal, they are still an awesome sight in flight with their mighty 7ft (2m) wingspan.

The best place to view bald eagles at any time is Alaska, but head to the Chilkat River close to Haines from October onward, and you will see a spectacular gathering of them. Over 3,000 eagles set up nest on one short stretch of river, lining the branches of surrounding cottonwood trees, or congregating on sandbars in readiness. This is one of the few places along the river that does not freeze, thanks to its gravel bottom which retains heat from warm summer water. It is also the spot where salmon that have spawned come to die.

Warm water plus dying salmon keeps these magnificent birds going through the long cold winter and you can watch them eating and squabbling—some have traveled from as far afield as Washington State for the bounty. Haines runs a two-day festival in mid-November where you can join guided viewings and watch wild rehabilitated eagles being released.

CANADA'S GREAT RAPTOR CONVENTION

At Brackendale in British Columbia, there's also a huge annual gathering of bald eagles, with excellent viewing opportunities from Cheakamus Valley to Squamish Estuary. The most popular view point is Eagle Viewing Dike and the best viewing time is usually from late December.

Meet the king of the apes

The plight of the mountain gorilla was made famous by Dian Fossey. Despite conservation efforts it remains one of the rarest animals on the planet. To see gorillas in the mist you need to journey to Central Africa.

GET CLOSE TO CHIMPANZEES

One of the best places to see chimps in the wild is at Greystoke Mahale on the eastern shore of Lake Tanganyika, Tanzania. This reserve in the valley behind the Mahale Mountains offers hiking trips to see what is thought to be the world's largest population of chimpanzees. It's a fabulously exotic location that also offers great swimming and sailing.

The mountain gorilla is critically endangered, a victim of deforestation, poaching, and, more recently, human conflict. Its fragile status makes even tourism a threat to this gentle giant's survival, so it's essential to check out the credentials of tour operators before you sign up for a gorilla watch. While it may be fine to observe these creatures from a respectful distance, close interaction may threaten their very existence.

Most gorilla safaris take place in Uganda/Rwanda around the Parc National des Volcans in the Virunga mountains, plus Mgahinga and Bwindi Impenetrable National Park. You are never guaranteed a sighting, and it can be an arduous trek through the misty forest, but catching sight of a family group of silverback is unforgettable. While their King Kong reputation persists, in reality these are gentle creatures who live sociably and peacefully, feasting on vegetation and the occasional insect. Aggression is usually between dominant males—and chest-beating is usually as far as it goes.

Get close to Europe's only primate

The Barbary ape is the only primate (apart from us) to live wild in Europe, and it has been a famous feature of Gibraltar for centuries. Some think the apes are the last survivors of a much larger European population.

Gibraltar is one of the last outposts of Europe and it's only 13 miles (21 km) across the Straits to North Africa. This might explain the origins of its population of Barbary apes, since they are also found in the Atlas Mountains of Morocco and northern Algeria. No one can explain exactly how or when they arrived on Gibraltar, although the most popular theory is that they were introduced by either the British or the Moors.

What is certain is that this small population of tailless and gregarious animals is cherished. Not only are they a major tourist attraction, but legend has it that if they leave Gibraltar, the Rock will fall. It's said that in World War II Winston Churchill gave strict instructions that a population of at least 24 should be maintained. These days, they are under the charge of the government of Gibraltar, which ensures a population of around 160 on the Upper Nature Reserve.

You'll have no trouble getting close to them—indeed they will come right up to you if they think there's a chance of being fed. This interaction is now discouraged by hefty fines, but you can still watch them playing and grooming each other. Best viewing is at Queen's Gate, also known as Apes' Den. Barbary apes in North Africa don't fare so well. With their habitat under threat because of logging, they are considered a vulnerable species, and appear on the IUCN Red List.

Watch lambs frolic at a rare breeds farm

Before farming became big business, wonderful varieties inhabited the farmyard. At Wimpole Hall you can not only enjoy a traditional farm setting, but watch a wild and wooly selection of lambs at play.

Counting sheep is far from sleep-inducing if you head to Wimpole Hall, a country house in Cambridgeshire with its own rare breeds farm attached. The thatched and timbered farm buildings seem worlds away from modern agri-business, where cattle, pigs, and sheep are look-alike strains bred for superior milk, meat, or wool production.

Down on this farm are Gloucester Old Spot pigs that any farmer would be proud to include in the family portrait, along with Irish moiled and longhorn cattle, bagot goats and shire horses. But it's the sheep that are the scene stealers. There are Manx Loaghtan, shaggy-coated Portlands, ancient Soays, and the critically endangered Norfolk horn. There's even the original black sheep, the Hebridean.

During lambing weekends in March and April you have a good chance of seeing lambs born and can watch these rare survivors of an earlier age frolicking among the spring flowers.

THE WORLD'S RAREST COW

Enderby Island cows were survivors of a 19th-century attempt to introduce farming to a sub-Antarctic island off New Zealand. After a century in splendid isolation munching seaweed, the herd was destroyed to restore the island's ecosystem. One heifer called Lady and her calf were rescued. Although the calf later died, Lady survived and became a national celebrity after she was successfully cloned. Breeding continues and it's hoped this unique variety can be saved.

Hear the call of the wolf

The gray wolf has had a negative press for centuries. Always the bad-guy in fairytales, it was driven to almost extinction in most of Europe and North America. However, recent conservation efforts may improve your chances of hearing one howl.

GET REAL CLOSE TO A KEYSTONE PREDATOR

The Wolf Conservation Center in South Salem, New York State offers educational tours where you learn about the history and ecology of the animals, meet "ambassador wolves" in an enclosure, or hike to see unenclosed packs during their evening howl.

The gray wolf was once the most widely distributed mammal apart from man. A combination of hunting and loss of natural terrain has seen their territory reduce dramatically. Wolf lovers (and there are many) say that the animal's reputation as a killer is unfounded, and it deserves to be part of our wild landscape. A similarly convinced anti-wolf group argues we are better off without a powerful predator that comes into conflict with man and livestock.

Populations survive in Canada and parts of Michigan and Wisconsin, and a reintroduction program has seen the wolf return to Yellowstone. Your best chance of seeing them here is to sign up for a Wolf Tracker program—a guided tour around the park in the company of trained wildlife guides.

In Europe, the wolf's fortunes are more mixed. While reintroduction into Scotland continues to be debated, there are still pockets in remote regions including Norway, Italy, and Spain. The largest European population is in the Carpathian Mountains of Romania, and several specialist vacation companies offer wildlife tours of the region.

CHAPTER 3

Thrills and Adventures

 Elegant race-meets, epic road journeys, or close encounters with elephants on safari—they are all here in a chapter dedicated to adventurous (and sometimes downright dangerous) pursuits.

We've covered famous and infamous festivals and sporting challenges, along with unique opportunities to test your own nerve, or watch other brave souls from the safety of the sidelines. Finally there are the thrills everyone can participate in—from crossing the world's highest bridge, to embarking on a magical mystery tour.

Hitch a ride in a fighter jet

The best place to experience the thrill of high-speed flight is at Cape Town's Thunder City, home of the world's largest private collection of classic jets fighters.

Adrenaline addicts fly to South Africa just to fly out again on a joy ride, because this is just about the only place on earth where you can ride in three of the most revered jet fighters of the Cold War years. The complex is next to Cape Town Airport, and was started by an aircraft enthusiast who bought his first jet as a "runaround."

Although you can buy similar extreme adventures in the US and some former Soviet countries, this beats them both for scenery—giving fabulous views over Table Mountain and the coast. It also offers a chance to participate in extreme aerobatics, since the skies south of the Cape are not so crowded with passenger aircraft.

You have to be prepared to dig deep because it costs a fortune to keep this fleet airworthy and pay the fuel bills. Past fliers have raided their bank accounts, and sold their cars just to experience the G-force and say they've sat in the cockpit of the last of a flying breed.

The planes themselves are legends. There's the Hawker Hunter, an air fighter that formed the backbone of the RAF from 1954 to 1995. For ground-hugging maneuvers at dizzying speed, opt for a seat in the BAe Buccaneer. Best for speed-freaks is the English Electric Lightning, a jet that guarantees your stomach remains at ground level when your body is heading for orbit. It climbs at over 50,000ft (15,200m) a minute to take you to an altitude where you can clearly see the curvature of the earth.

Loop the loop in a biplane

You are guaranteed the full Biggles experience if you dare to take to the skies in the open cockpit of a vintage biplane once used to train fighter pilots. Chocks away!

While the celebrated Spitfire is a rare sight in flight, and few members of the public get to ride in one these days, it's perfectly possible to take to the skies above Britain in an even older bird from the 1930s. This is flying as God intended it—sun in your eyes, wind in your face, and a distinctly small and vulnerable feeling when you look down at the hard and unforgiving ground below.

One of the best locations to relive the glory days of early flight is Gloucestershire Airport—formerly Staverton—and once home of the legendary Gloster Aircraft Company. Here Tiger Airways organizes joyrides for novice fliers in Tiger Moths, Boeing Stearman, and the Belgian Stampe SV4. Really brave would-be fliers can sign up for a short course in aerobatics, flying a modern military trainer called the Firefly, and learning a few moves to scare loved ones watching from the ground below.

Or GRAB a seat in a Spitfire

Tiger Airways can also arrange flights on a US-owned Spitfire (a rare opportunity now that only around 50 are left in existence). This is not a cheap pastime since you have to travel to New York for a 45-minute joyride. For aficionados, it may well be worth the expense, since the plane has dual controls, and the owner is willing to try a few aerobatics as long as the passenger is up for it.

Climb up the world's steepest street

You have to be super-fit or a masochist to attempt to scale Baldwin Street, Dunedin—officially listed in the record books as the steepest paved street in the world. Your calf muscles may never recover.

In fact New Zealand contains plenty of masochists, since there's an annual race up and then down Baldwin Street known as the "Gut Buster." The fact that the street was constructed in this way is reputed to be the result of a planning oversight—it was mapped out almost 12,000 miles (19,300km) away in the UK by town planners who were more concerned with creating an orderly grid plan than sparing the legs of local residents.

The result is, to say the least, challenging, as in places the gradient is 1 in 2.86. Because of the dizzying climb, you are strongly advised not to drive up the street. Anyone who does should only attempt it in very low gear and do their best to avoid an engine stall as rolling downhill can be swift and terrifying.

TWO MORE HARD ROADS TO CLIMB

1. HARLECH UNDRIVEABLE (IT'S STRICTLY FOR WALKERS OR MOUNTAIN BIKERS), FFORDD PENLLECH IS A TWISTING LANE THAT LEADS UPHILL FROM THE CENTER OF THIS HISTORICAL CITY IN NORTH-WESTERN WALES. THE GRADIENT IS 1 IN 2.5.

2. SAN FRANCISCO THE MOST FAMOUS HILLS IN THE CITY ARE ON THE CITY'S CABLE-CAR ROUTES. THESE ARE NOT THE STEEPEST THOUGH. HEAD TO FILBERT STREET BETWEEN HYDE AND LEAVENWORTH, OR 22ND STREET BETWEEN CHURCH AND VICKSBURG. ON BOTH STREETS THE GRADIENT REACHES 1 IN 1.85.

Travel a deadly route

Bolivia's El Camino de la Muerte (which translates as Road of Death) is not the most relaxing of tourist highlights. But there are plenty of brave adventurers willing to see if they can cheat *la muerte*.

This road links the Andean mountains above the capital La Paz with the town of Coroico. It is infamous among truck drivers and locals, but has become something of a badge of courage for independent travelers. The most popular way for tourists to travel the route and live to tell the tale is to join a mountain-biking group. This death-defying journey begins at over 16,000ft (4,875m) above sea level and descends for 43 miles in a series of hairpin bends to bring you into lush rain forest. The views are stunning, and since the dirt road is only ten feet wide with no guard rails, there are plenty of opportunities to contemplate your mortality along the way.

Be warned though, the annual death rate has been as high as 150 along this one small stretch of road. Crosses, altars, and tire tracks disappearing over the edge are a salutary reminder to test your brakes at regular intervals. There are so many blind bends that there are reports of kind-hearted locals standing at the side of the road waving red and green flags and acting as "human traffic lights."

This is the only road in Bolivia where you drive on the left—a degree of reassurance if you're hugging the inside edge on the trek uphill, but not half so comforting on the journey downhill.

Head to the world's greatest rodeos

The US gave us John Wayne, but Canada also has a proud wild-west heritage to celebrate. So would-be cowboys and cowgirls should grab their boots and visit two of the biggest North American rodeos.

As home of Davie Crockett and the Alamo, it's only fitting that Texas should host the big one—and Houston Livestock Show and Rodeo each February ticks all the boxes. The three-week festival is very much a working show, with the world's largest livestock exhibition. Preceding the event there are trail rides from Texas and beyond, bringing visitors to the show on horseback to recreate the atmosphere of the Old West. The rodeo competitions take place in a huge indoor arena, with other events such as parades and barbecue cook-offs in Reliant Park. Traditionally, this event has also showcased huge stars—Elvis Presley once topped the bill—and it routinely attracts over two million visitors.

The second most famous rodeo is north of the border in Alberta. Calgary Stampede each July is an extravaganza in honor of Canada's frontier heritage. This is your golden opportunity to dress up as a cowboy, gorge on corn dogs and pancakes with maple syrup, and watch rodeo and the even more dangerous chuckwagon racing. These days, Calgary is a boom town fueled by oil, but still the celebration of its past draws in crowds of well over a million. Competitions include bronc riding, steer wrestling, and team roping, with prize money for the professional rodeo riders topping the million-dollar mark.

Compete in the cheese-rolling Olympics

The annual Cheese Rolling and Wake in Gloucestershire is a one-of-a-kind dangerous sport that anyone is free to enter—although it helps to be brave or foolish or both.

Each May holiday, competitors and spectators assemble at Cooper's Hill, a perilous descent in a field off the main road between Cheltenham and Stroud. Anyone over 18 is free to enter and the object is simple: chase a giant cheese down a hill. There is a catch though—the hill is so steep that it's almost impossible to stay upright.

The event begins when a "guest roller" starts the cheese on its course down the hill. Then, at a signal from the master of ceremonies, the competitors chase after it. The first to get to the bottom wins the big cheese—a 7lb (3kg) handcrafted Double Gloucester truckle made locally. There are four races, including one ladies' event, and it's fiercely competitive with entrants from as far afield as New Zealand.

Unfortunately, due to the 2:1 gradient (1:1 in places) the toll of casualties can be high. The worst casualty list in recent memory was recorded as 33. Most injuries are sprains or cuts, and volunteer ambulance teams and paramedics wait at the bottom to tend to the injured. The organizing committee does what it can to make the hill safe in the weeks before the event—clearing scrub and nettles, erecting safety fences and straw-bale crash barriers. Sometimes spectators don't get off lightly either—one was hit by a bouncing cheese with such tremendous force that he tumbled down the hill after it.

FOUR MORE RACES TO CHALLENGE YOU

1. HENLEY-ON-TODD An Australian spoof of the famous British regatta, this Alice Springs competition includes a bath-tub derby, white-water kayak, and battle-boat spectacular. All events take place on sand (desert equals no river), and in some races the boats are carried.

2. . WIFE-CARRYING WORLD CHAMPIONSHIP Sonkajärvi in Finland hosts this race. You carry your own or someone else's as long as she's over 17 years old and weighs at least 108lb (49kg). The 277yd (253m) course includes a challenging water obstacle. Wife-dropping incurs a 15-second time penalty.

3. WORLD BOG TRIATHLON The Welsh town of Llanwrtyd Powys hosts the ultimate challenge each August —a 12 mile (19km) fell or mountain run, 19 mile (31km) mountain-bike ride, and, worst of all, a 120yd (110m) swim through a dense and smelly peat bog. Snorkel and fins are allowed but the only swimming stroke competitors can use is the dog paddle.

4. WORLD BEARD AND MOUSTACHE GROWING CHAMPIONSHIP A biennial event held in a different hotbed of hirsute activity around the globe (Anchorage, Alaska is next in line). You need patience and a good crop of facial hair, and categories include the Dali, Sideburns Freestyle, and Musketeer. There are strict rules on tricks with false hair and extensions.

Join the running of the bulls

This dangerous participation event takes place in Pamplona, as part of the town's Feast of San Fermin. The bulls are far from docile, and each year there are scores of injuries as people get too close to the animals' horns or hoofs.

Pamplona's nine-day festival (July 6–14) in honor of its patron saint can be a gory business. While local residents may focus on the fireworks, the parade, or the partying, there is only one thing many visitors want to do—risk their lives by outrunning the bulls. The event, which happens early in the morning, and only takes around three minutes, attracts mixed crowds of athletes and romantics, and the resulting injuries that some of them incur can be life-threatening.

The bulls are not your lumbering farmyard breed, but championship athletes, weighing in at up to half a ton (600kg), and are bred specifically for bullfighting. Their short run through the twisting streets of Pamplona is a prelude to the gory spectacle that takes place each evening in the city's huge bullring.

You can blame Pamplona's popularity on Ernest Hemingway, who made bull running—known locally as *el encierro*—famous with a description of Pamplona's fiesta in the novel *The Sun Also Rises*. Back then, this Basque city was a sleepy place, but now over a million people attend during the feast, making accommodation almost impossible to find. If you do join the running, the local advice if you fall over on the slippery cobbles is to cover your head, play dead, and try not to attract the attention of a passing *toro*.

Take an African elephant safari

Getting up close to these majestic creatures is an experience in itself, but if you head to South Africa, you can climb on the back of an elephant, and see the surrounding wildlife from a whole new angle.

Climbing on the back of a six-ton animal that could crush you with one stamp of its foot can be a daunting experience. But don't let that put you off. Elephant safaris are an increasingly popular way of seeing the countryside in South Africa, Botswana, and Zambia because not only do you have a bird's-eye view of the savanna or jungle, but you also get closer to other wildlife than you would in a jeep or on foot. This is because the scent of an elephant tends to overpower that of a human.

Most safaris take place in game reserves, and the sunrise and sunset tours are best for game-viewing and heat avoidance. You have an experienced elephant driver holding the reins and, although it isn't the most comfortable ride, there's a saddle to hold on to, so the best thing to do is relax, and enjoy the sights and sounds of the veldt.

OR SEE THAILAND FROM AN ELEPHANT'S BACK

Elephants were once the main form of transportation in the hill country of northern Thailand, and are still the best way to experience the jungle. Chang Mai and Chang Rai are popular starting points, and you can also hitch a ride with farming elephants around Sangkhla Buri close to the Burmese border. These Asian elephants are not so lofty as their African cousins, but it's still a long way down to the ground.

Ride on an ostrich

If you visit Safari Ostrich Show Farm in Oudtshoorn, South Africa you can learn more about the life of the planet's largest bird, and even try the unusual sport of ostrich-riding.

Ostrich farming dates back to the 1880s and during the heydey of seriously large hats for ladies, South Africa's exports of feathers ranked fourth after gold, diamonds, and wool. These days, ostriches are more prized for their meat and hides, but you can still pick up a feather boa at the ostrich farming capital Oudtshoorn.

It's the live ostriches that most visitors come to see and a tour of the farm shows you every stage of their development, from giant eggs to fully grown birds standing up to 9ft (2.7m) tall. During the breeding season you can also visit the incubation room and watch chicks hatch. The highlight is the Ostrich Derby in which skilled local jockeys race the giant birds. They may not match thoroughbred horses but can reach speeds of up to 40mph (65kmh) over a short stretch. If you're brave enough, you can even try it yourself. The mounts selected are semi-tame—riding the rest of the herd is not recommended as they can deliver a vicious kick.

DO OSTRICHES BURY THEIR HEADS?

The old saying about ostriches is curious, since no one has ever recorded them burying their heads in the sand. However, they do have a couple of quirks. When threatened by predators, they lie down flat with necks outstretched to blend in with the background. They also consume quantities of grit and pebbles to aid digestion, which may explain why they sometimes appear to have their heads in the sand.

Head to an ancient horse festival

Nadaam is an annual celebration based around the ancient Mongol warrior pursuits of horse racing, wrestling, and archery. For visitors it's a chance to watch feats of athletic prowess and experience a great nomadic culture.

Each year between July 11 and 13, the whole of Mongolia stops work to celebrate its three national sports in a huge and colorful festival. While the biggest and most famous celebration is in the capital Ulaan Baatar, this is a participation event in every town and village. It is not just the men who compete—women and children also participate in the archery and horse-racing.

One of the most spectacular events is the first day parade, in which athletes, monks, and other people dressed just like Genghis Khan (or Chinggis Khan to use the preferred spelling) march to the capital's main stadium for the grand opening ceremony.

The horse-racing is the main draw for Western visitors. Mongolians start riding as babes-in-arms, but nothing quite prepares you for the sight of a small child (maybe as young as five) riding a 12-mile (20-km) race bareback. The racing takes place a short distance outside the capital, and many mounts and their jockeys have trained for months and traveled vast distances to attend. You may see as many as 400 animals competing in each event—an awesome sight as they gallop across the plain.

The crush surrounding the competitions all adds to the atmosphere, with families descending on the capital to camp out, have a barbecue, and enjoy traditions that seem miles away from the Soviet-era skyscrapers that dominate the city's skyline.

Experience great horse-racing

Whether you attend for the social atmosphere or the thrill of hoofs pounding on turf, there's a date in the calendar to suit everyone. Here are four great excuses to buy a plane ticket and an outrageous hat.

1. March, Dubai Gold Cup

The richest horse-racing prize in the world, this race on the last Saturday in March attracts billionaires, sheikhs, and the seriously glamorous to Nad Al Sheba racetrack. It's worth going the extra mile on your outfits as the annual Style Stakes competition awards holidays and shopping sprees to the best dressed.

2. May, Kentucky Derby

Dating back to 1875, this hallowed event at Churchill Downs, Louisville takes place on the first Saturday in May, marking the end of two weeks of racing. Millionaire's Row is where the racing fraternity rub shoulders with Hollywood A-Listers (some pretty unlikely stars own their own horses), and everyone drinks mint juleps.

3. June, Royal Ascot

Sandwiched between the Derby and Glorious Goodwood, this six-day meet in Ascot, Berkshire is the highlight of the social season for serious racegoers, but also attracts hordes of spectators who just want to dress up and enjoy. Ladies' Day is when the serious (and sometimes silly) hats come out. Gourmet picnics in the car park are just as time-honored a tradition as see-and-be-seen around the Parade Ring.

4. November, Melbourne Cup

Run on the first Tuesday in November, this event sets all Australia into a fever as bets are placed to see who will win the country's richest horse-racing prize. The distance and handicap make it hard to predict—all adding to the fun for the 100,000 or so fans at Flemington raceground.

Join the world's glamorous car rally

Gumball 3000 is the ultimate thrills-and-spills racing adventure as classic cars and celebrity drivers cross international borders by automobile—and sometimes plane—in an epic 3,000 mile journey.

This modern-day Wacky Races takes inspiration from a classic coast-to-coast trek across the USA that later became immortalized in the film *Cannonball Run*. The big difference with Gumball 3000 is that the route changes each year, the 3,000 mile (5,000km) journey takes more than a week and entrants have to pack their party clothes.

Competitors have included music and film stars, the cast of *Jackass,* and even a Great Train Robber. Members of the public can form their own teams, although it costs around $60,000 for the privilege—which explains the high percentage of rich and famous among the entrants. The vehicles are almost as eye-catching as the racers, and have included everything from Rolls Royce Phantoms and Ferrari Enzos, to the General Lee (of *Dukes of Hazzard* fame), and a cumbersome but homey Winnebago RV.

The first race in 1999 took a somewhat roundabout route from London, via Italy, France, and Austria, to Hockenheim Grand Prix Circuit in Germany. Subsequent routes have included Paris to Marrakech, London to LA (including a Trans-Atlantic plane ride), and a trek across Europe to Asia. In honor of Gumball's 10th anniversary in 2008, the route is London to Sydney.

Glamor is as essential as driving and navigational skills, so road-weary entrants check into luxurious hotels and castles each evening, unwrap their finery and prepare to party all night—just one more element of this extreme test of stamina.

Drive the world's tallest bridge

A spectacular feat of engineering, Millau Viaduct is a cable-stayed bridge spanning the Tarn River valley in southern France. Designed to ease vacation traffic, it has become a tourist sight in itself.

Le Viaduc de Millau has become one of the sights of the South of France. Opened in 2004, and designed by architects Foster and Partners and structural engineer Dr Michel Virlogeux, it entered the record books as the world's tallest vehicular bridge because

EIGHT GREAT TECHNICAL FEATS TO CROSS

1. AKASHI-KAIKYO
This six-lane highway links Japan's Awaji Island with Kobe, bypassing a notoriously treacherous stretch of water. It's an impressive suspension design with a 6,530ft (1,990m) distance between its center spans.

2. BLOUKRANS
A spectacular setting in Nature's Valley, Western Cape makes this arched bridge in South Africa particularly photogenic. Standing 709ft (216m) above the river, it won awards for its ingenious use of concrete.

3. CONFEDERATION
This concrete box-girder bridge links Prince Edward Island with New Brunswick. It's a journey of around 8 miles (13km) across the Northumberland Strait, and the bridge is officially part of the Trans-Canada Highway.

4. DONGHAI
Over 20 miles (32km) long, this gargantuan structure entered the record books as the world's longest sea bridge when it opened in 2005. It links the city of Shanghai with Yangshan port.

one of its seven concrete piers stands a mighty 804ft (245m) tall. The eight-lane steel roadway forms a long arc high above the valley floor, allowing traffic to bypass the medieval town of Millau.

The bridge has been recognized as an amazing technical feat, but it is also an inspiring design. Each of its seven piers is topped with a 295ft (90m) cable-stayed mast, giving it an elegant sail-like profile that looks particularly impressive when it's illuminated at night. Travelers speeding between Clermont-Ferrand and Béziers, or driving onward to Spain have reason to be grateful on two counts: first, the bridge has cut the journey time by four hours in peak vacation season; and second, it has added to the appeal of this beautiful river valley.

5. ØRESUNDSBRON

Linking Denmark and Sweden, this bridge-tunnel crosses the Oresund Strait. It's both a major route in Europe, and is its longest combined road-and-railroad bridge.

6. SUNSHINE SKYWAY

The world's longest cable-stayed concrete bridge, this crosses Tampa Bay, Florida, connecting St Petersburg with Palmetto. It has recently been renamed Bob Graham Sunshine Skyway Bridge in honor of the Florida governor who presided over its construction.

7. SYDNEY HARBOR

An iconic symbol of the city, the "Coathanger" celebrated its 75th birthday in 2007. It was an ambitious design that still retains records as the largest steel-arch bridge and the widest long-span bridge.

8. VASCO DE GAMA

A six-lane freeway across the Tagus River, this bridge north of Lisbon opened in 1998 and involved more than 3,000 workers in its construction. At almost 11 miles (18km) long it's an awesome engineering feat.

Experience great endurance races

For thrill-seeking motorists, here are three more great tests that promise exotic foreign travel, bad roads, team camaraderie, and plenty of sand in your eyes.

1. Dakar Rally

The Dakar, as it's known in racing circles, is one of the ultimate road adventures. It is also one of the few leading motor-racing events where amateurs make up the bulk of competitors. It started in 1978 as a run from Paris to the Senegalese port of Dakar, but later shifted its official starting point, and since 2006 it has begun in Lisbon. Motorcycles, cars, and trucks all compete, and the most testing sections of the 5,500 mile (8,900km) course are the Western Sahara and the Adrar Plateau in Mauritania.

2. Baja 1000

This off-road race in Mexico is open to motorcycles, but a four-wheel drive is handy on the rough terrain. The usual course runs from Ensenada to La Paz and is around 1,000 miles (1,600km). The biggest hazards along the route are the holes or obstacles spectators sometimes add to the course to maximize the roadside entertainment.

3. Plymouth—Banjul Challenge

This testing three-week race for the hard-up and certifiable has been run since 2003, originally to Dakar, but now to the capital of the Gambia. The most crucial rule is that competing cars must cost less than $200 to buy and pre-rally modifications have a maximum ceiling of $30. This means some hapless entrants barely make it beyond British shores in their bangers. Those vehicles that do triumphantly reach the finish line having braved desert sandstorms and breakdowns are auctioned off for Gambian charities.

Go skiing in the desert

Perhaps it's human nature to want what we don't have. While residents of chilly northern Europe or the US may yearn for the sun, some inhabitants of sweltering Dubai hanker after pristine white snow.

It may be sweltering outside, but if you head to Ski Dubai you can get an almost authentic Alpine chill through your bones. You can even stay in accommodation that overlooks the piste. This is the third-largest indoor ski slope in the world with five runs of varying difficulty. The longest is 1,300ft (400m) with a 197ft (60m) descent.

The complex uses home-produced real snow and offers ski lifts, loan of winter clothing, and ski gear, or snowboarding kit and lessons. There's also a dedicated snowman-building zone for over-excited children and adults. For an almost-authentic alpine experience, visitors can stay in the Kempinski Hotel overlooking the slopes. Deluxe ski chalets offer the spectacle of alpine views on one side, and desert and beach on the other.

While this is ambitious, it is nothing compared with Dubai Sunny Mountain Ski Dome, opening in 2008. Along with an artificial mountain range, snow maze, ice slide, and revolving ski slope, it promises genuine polar bears.

VISIT EUROPE'S BIGGEST INDOOR COMPLEX

Europe's largest indoor ski resort is in the Netherlands—a country challenged not so much by lack of snow as a distinct lack of mountains to ski down. The Skicenter Snow World complex at Landgraaf in Limburg province has three slopes—two of them 1,700ft (520m) long—and offers skiing as well as tube gliding and airboarding.

Enjoy fever pitch

Even if you've never played baseball, Fenway Park is one of an elite group of stadiums around the world where it's worth the price of a ticket just to savor the atmosphere.

The home of the Boston Red Sox, Fenway Park is the smallest, oldest, and most expensive place to watch baseball in the majors. The seats are uncomfortable and some views are blocked by columns. It has a reputation for being unlucky, because it opened in 1912 in the same week that the Titanic went down. There's even said to be a curse on the team because after selling Babe Ruth they didn't win the World Series for 86 years.

So why bother? Perhaps adversity makes you stronger—or crazier—because this is home to some of the most passionate baseball nuts in North America. It also has the aura of a shrine, with its famous Green Monster (a wall), and the Lone Red Seat, marking the point of the longest home run. Tradition, passion, and fantastically loyal fans—what more do you need for a great afternoon's entertainment?

FOUR MORE STADIUMS WITH UNBEATABLE ATMOSPHERE

1. STADIWM Y MILIENIWM

The Millenium Stadium rose phoenix-like from the ashes of the old Cardiff Arms Park and is the spiritual and physical home of Welsh rugby. It sits in the heart of the capital—unusual for such a large venue—and although it's a shiny new building with a retractable roof, it still retains the atmosphere of its predecessor. The passionate pre-match singing has been known to make grown men weep.

2. MARACANÃ, BRAZIL

On a continentwild about soccer, this Rio de Janeiro colossus has achieved an almost mythical status. It was built to host the 1950 World Cup final and an amazing 220,000 people attended the match that local rival Uruguay has never been forgiven for winning. A must for the crowd atmosphere and the knowledge that so many soccer legends have played here.

3. MELBOURNE CRICKET GROUND

The newly refurbished MCG has a 100,000 capacity making it Australia's largest sporting venue. This was the stage for the first ever Test Match in 1877. and the annual Boxing Day meet is an Australian tradition. It is also used for the Australian Rules Grand Final, rugby and football events. The atmosphere generated by the local crowd has an uncanny knack of subduing visiting teams.

4. FNB SOCCER CITY, SOUTH AFRICA

It may not be on everyone's list yet, but this Johannesburg stadium was built to accommodate the biggest and fastest-growing sport in South Africa. Opened in 1989, renovation will increase its capacity to 94,700 in time for the 2010 World Cup. It has already hosted hallowed events (it's where Nelson Mandela gave his first speech outside Cape Town after his prison release), and is certain to be the venue for many more.

Combine ski and beach

Talk about running hot and cold—morning on the piste and afternoon on the beach. While the combination in Dubai is artificial, here are five natural settings where you can do both in one action-packed day.

1. Canada

Head to Vancouver for fabulous diving, swimming, or sailing, and then take the "Sea to Sky Highway" (Highway 99) to get to Whistler, a year-round ski resort with open-glacier skiing and more than 200 marked trails.

2. California

At Pomona College, access to snow and surf is so celebrated that students hold an annual celebration in early spring, starting off at Mountain High Resort in Wrightwood and finishing with a swim and beach barbecue. The resort is also handy for residents of LA and San Diego.

3. Cyprus

Head to this eastern Mediterranean island in the winter and you can ski or snowboard on Mount Olympus in the Troodos Mountains, and be back at your poolside for cocktails in the afternoon. February and March are the best months for snow and at that time of the year you may be basking in 70° fahrenheit (20° celsius) down by the sea.

4. Lebanon

Once known as the Switzerland of the Mid East, Lebanon has several ski resorts to choose from, the best known being Faraya Mzaar. This offers views down to the much balmier coast from a lofty 8,100ft (2,465m) peak. The ski season mimics that in the Alps, lasting for around four months.

5. Morocco

Oukaimeden Ski Resort at 8,700ft (2,650m) in the majestic Atlas mountains is clearly visible from Marrakech, making it possible to combine a spell of alpine adventure with leisurely strolls around the sun-baked Medina.

Visit the most scenic ice-skating rinks

Ice skating has to be one of the most idyllic of winter activities. Wrap up warm, master those blades, and then make a few gentle circuits before taking a break for hot chocolate or mulled wine. Here are some top spots to practice your figure of eight.

1. Central Park, New York
Manhattan has a choice of locations, with Wollman Rink on the East Side at 62nd Street, and Lasker Rink up at 106th Street. Both are open from November to the end of March, and lay on music as well as (hopefully) perfect crisp winter weather.

2. City Park, Budapest
A boating lake in the center of Városliget becomes a giant skating rink over the winter. It's a stunning venue—the largest outdoor rink in Central Europe—and has great views over Vajdahunyad Castle.

3. Leidseplein, Amersterdam
You can skate for free on a frozen canal right in the heart of Amsterdam from mid-November to early January. Skates can be hired on site and there are stalls selling mini pancakes around this picturesque rink.

4. Montreal, Canada
The whole of Montreal goes winter crazy during La Fête des Neiges each January and February. Along with ice sculpture, skiing, and tube-sliding, you can skate outdoors along the Île Sainte Helene, giving great views of downtown Montreal.

5. Somerset House, London
The courtyard outside London's Somerset House close to the Thames becomes a magical venue for ice skating in the run-up to Christmas (usually staying open until the end of January). Evening skating sessions are best because the courtyard is illuminated.

Travel the world's longest ski run

The Vallée Blanche is considered by many to be the greatest of all ski runs. Beginning in the mountains above Chamonix, it descends more than 13.7 miles (22km) to the valley floor below.

The Vallée Blanche is heaven for skiers—provided the snow and blue skies have put in an appearance. Not only do you have stunning Alpine scenery from the summit at Aiguille du Midi, but an enormous winter playground stretches down the mountain side ahead of you. The ride up the valley via the cable car is the first thrill, and once at the top you can see clearly across the border into France and Italy.

This is not a run for beginners—not even experienced skiers should attempt it without a mountain guide because it is off-piste glacier skiing, which means you need someone with you who really understands the terrain, and is familiar with local weather and snow hazards. Although ski-fiends say this is not the world's most challenging run, it does require stamina (it's around a four-hour journey) and control to navigate your way around some of the trickier sections.

You are advised to pick a sunny and calm day so you can enjoy the views and avoid the biting winds that can assail you at the start of the run. Also remember to get there early—this is a popular "been-there-done-that" challenge for skiers from around the globe.

The reward once you've made it back to Chamonix for well-deserved après-ski is to know that you have completed one of the most epic—and famous—winter sports challenges in the world.

Cheer on BASE jumpers

Perhaps the world's most extreme sport, BASE jumping involves throwing yourself off a high point, and then opening your parachute in the nick of time. You can see it—legally—at Bridge Day in West Virginia.

The 876ft (267m) descent is dizzying, and with just seconds to get that parachute open there is absolutely no margin for error. It's a heart-in-mouth moment looking over the parapet to the fast-moving water below—and that's just for the spectators. No wonder the atmosphere at one of the few legal BASE jumping festivals in the USA is electric; where else can you watch people cheat death with such aplomb? The event takes place at New River Gorge Bridge, Fayetteville annually on the third Saturday in October, and attracts around 450 competitors and 200,000 spectators.

You can understand why governments and authorities are slow to embrace BASE (which stands for the four jumping possibilities of Building, Antenna, Span, Earth). It is dangerous—madness even—because one wrong move and you are dead. Illegal BASE jumping takes place anyway, from bridges, high points in Yosemite, and even off the top of city-center buildings. Those who survive the jump face possible arrest—so they are usually deadly serious about their sport!

NORWAY'S EXTREME DISPLAYS

Kjerag are spectacular mountains 3,280ft (1,000m) above the southern end of Lysefjord, Norway that welcome BASE jumpers. You can find them there throughout the summer months and even if you're not lucky enough to catch a parachute display, it's a spectacular beauty spot. Sightseeing boats run from Stavanger to towns and villages around the fjord.

Tackle the Seven Summits

The ultimate mountaineering challenge is to climb the highest peaks on seven continents. If Everest (see page 7) just whets your appetite, here are the other climbs you need to complete to earn your crampons.

Africa

Actually a stratavaro (an inactive volcano), Kilimanjaro in north eastern Tanzania stands 19,340ft (5,895m) tall at its main summit Kibo. It has the highest rise of any mountain— 15,000ft (4,600m) from the base.

Antarctica

Part of Antarctica's Sentinel mountain range, Vinson Massif was only discovered in 1957 when it was spotted from a US Navy aircraft. Its highest point Mount Craddock is 16,066ft (4,897m) tall.

Europe

The highest peak depends on where you place the border between Europe and Asia. The West Summit of Mount Elbrus in the Caucus mountains of Russia carries the crown for height, standing 18,442ft (5,642m) tall. But some scientists and geographers consider this mountain to be within the sphere of Asia, making Mont Blanc or Monte Blanco in the Graian Alps the highest climb of the European continent. Its summit is at 15,774ft (4,808m).

North America

Mount McKinley in Alaska stands about halfway between Anchorage and Fairbanks and is 20,320ft (6,194m) tall. Its name in Alaska and among mountaineers is Denali, which means "the Great One."

Oceania

There are two choices, depending on whose list you adhere to. Kosciuszko (7,310ft/2,228m) is in the New South Wales region known as the Australian Alps. Meanwhile Puncak Jaya on New

WHERE TO GET INTO TRAINING

1. BEN NEVIS A walk in the park compared with the Seven Summits, the UK's highest peak is just 4,406ft (1,344m) above sea level. Many visitors walk up the trail from Glen Nevis, but mountaineers find the north-facing cliffs a challenging training ground.

2. EIGER This mountain in the Swiss Alps is famous because it was one of the first to attract climbers, and the infamously sheer North Face was only successfully tackled in 1938. These days, the major risk is from rock falls as parts of the summit are crumbling quite badly.

3. MATTERHORN Straddling the Italian/Swiss border, this majestic peak inspired fear in early climbers because of its sheer faces. Frequent poor weather at the summit, and the risk of rock falls and avalanches make it a testing climb—the southern face being the toughest challenge.

4. MOUNT THOR Located on Baffin Island in Nunavut, northern Canada, Thor has the longest vertical cliff-face in the world, with an average angle of 105°. It is a formidable technical challenge for even the most experienced climbers.

Guinea is 16,535ft (5,040m) tall. Mountaineers often refer to it by its old name of Carstensz Pyramid.

South America

Aconcagua in the Argentinian Andes is considered an "easy" mountain because its southerly latitude means oxygen isn't required. The 22,834ft (6,960m) peak has been climbed in under six hours.

Watch cliff-diving supremos

Acapulco's *clavadistas* are famous—but while these brave souls may appear *loco* to watching bystanders, this is an elite gang of divers who train hard to create a fabulous tourist show.

Legend has it that cliff diving started because local fisherman would dive 130ft (40m) into La Quebrada—which literally translates as "the gorge"—to free trapped lines. It's an extreme way to sort out the fishing nets perhaps, but one that has entranced visitors to the Mexican resort since the 1930s.

These days it's a well regulated affair. The divers pray at a small shrine to the Virgin of Guadeloupe before they walk to the jumping point, and then choose their moment (the waves have got to be just right), and launch themselves into space. There's a viewing platform where you can watch for a small charge, but the most comfortable option is to take a seat in El Mirador Hotel. Although this makes a classic photo opportunity during the day, evening shows take place illuminated by flaring torches.

AMATEUR NIGHT AT RICK'S

Part of the fun of sundowners at Rick's Café in Negril, Jamaica is that amateurs and pros alike try cliff diving. This is not the extreme feat you watch at Acapulco since the cliff is only 33ft (10m) above the waves, but it is still high enough to make a badly executed dive dangerous as well as painful. Amateurs are advised to go feet-first, not head-first, although the watching crowd, fueled by rum cocktails, may secretly hope for a couple of resounding bellyflops.

Explore the deep in an underwater craft

With famously clear waters and an abundance of marine life, the Cayman Islands is a diver's paradise. But the ultimate adventure is to take a submarine journey down the reef wall.

It's a far cry from the cramped conditions of the submarines we remember from war movies, because these hybrid tourist craft are air-conditioned, pressure controlled, and give you a prime view of a tropical underwater environment through their large windows. The original model, *Atlantis 1*, was launched in Grand Cayman in the crystal clear waters of the Caribbean in 1986, and its successors are still operating today.

The submarine can carry 48 passengers to a depth of just over 100ft (30m) to get a close-up view of barrel sponges, star coral, and tropical groupers and snappers. More exotic still are the after-dark cruises. You see a completely different colorscape as iridescent night fishes come out to feed, and the reef is illuminated by the submarine's headlights.

The person behind the Atlantis Adventures submarines got the idea while working with equipment used to inspect oil-drilling rigs in the chilly (and exceedingly cloudy) waters of the North Sea. Now the company operates a variety of submersibles and semi-submersibles at more than a dozen tourist resorts around the Caribbean, Mexico, Hawaii, and Guam—and can boast that its fleet exceeds that of many national navies.

Go deeper still in a yellow submarine

The Bay Islands off Honduras are home to rich underwater life, and brave visitors can journey way beyond the limits of a scuba dive in an extraordinary custom-built sub.

Visitors to the scuba diving resort of Half Moon Bay on the island of Roatan can take the ultimate Heath Robinson-style journey aboard the mini-submersible *Idabel*. This lovingly engineered craft was built by Captain Karl Stanley of Stanley Submarines.

The custom-built yellow submarine has space on board for three people and can dive to a mighty depth of 2,000ft (610m) down the Cayman Trench. She has a large viewing bubble and in-sub music system to make the ride to the deep even more atmospheric. Her diminutive size means she is easy to navigate around coral cliffs, and can home in on unusual features such as sea lilies and giant sea sponges. Once you get to the inky depths around 1,800 ft (548m), the sub's lights pick out bizarre, sometimes prehistoric, animal and plant forms including sharks without dorsal fins and swimming sea cucumbers.

This is the second sub Captain Karl has built—he started crafting them when he was just 15—and he's renowned as a pioneer when it comes to underwater exploration. The sub's safety features (useful information for the nervous submariner) include three-days' supply of air and a large, lead weight that can be dropped in an emergency to give *Idabel* enough buoyancy to send her climbing back to the surface.

See Strawberry Fields

One of the Beatles' most evocative songs is also a real location that you can track down in Liverpool today. More atmospheric still is the special area of Central Park, New York that honors both the song and the man behind it.

TAKE A MAGICAL MYSTERY TOUR

Bus tours around Liverpool are the easiest way for Beatles fans to take in the essential sights, including the Strawberry Field gates and the addresses of Ringo and George. You can also book a tour around Paul's childhood home in Forthlin Road, and John's in Menlove Avenue since both are now National Trust properties.

This nostalgic song is based on John Lennon's memories of his Liverpool childhood. He sometimes used to play in the grounds of a Salvation Army children's home called Strawberry Field in Woolton—just around the corner from the home he shared with his Aunt Mimi. The distinctive gates leading to the Victorian mansion are on every Beatles fan's tour of the city, although the future of the children's home is in doubt since an announcement by the Salvation Army that it is scheduled to close. It seems certain that, whatever the fate of the building itself, the famous gates will be preserved.

A permanent memorial to the song can also be found in New York's Central Park. John Lennon and wife Yoko Ono lived at the Dakota Building, near this part of the park, and after Lennon's death it was renamed Strawberry Fields, and a new Garden of Peace was created by landscape architect Bruce Kelly. Plants were donated by 150 nations, and a mosaic in the pathway bears the single word "Imagine," after another one of Lennon's most revered songs.

Experience the ultimate high-speed event

Bonneville Salt Flats is a mecca for adrenalin junkies, and every year they congregate in a collection of bizarre vehicles to challenge land-speed records, and experience the thrill of pounding down one of the world's straightest and flattest natural racing courses.

Like something from a sci-fi movie, Bonneville Salt Flats near Wendover, Utah is a dazzling white landscape covering an area of over 30,000 acres. Once this contained a body of water equivalent to Lake Michigan. Now it's a vast mud basin covered with a crust of salt. In the winter, the area is covered with a thin layer of water, but as the temperature rises this evaporates, and the wind levels the salt to create a rock-hard surface.

Despite the harsh conditions, Bonneville has become famous for feats of high adventure. The first automobile speed record attempt took place in 1914, when Teddy Tetzlaff managed almost 142mph in a Blitzen Benz. In the 1930s British land-speed supremo Sir Malcolm Campbell was tempted across the Atlantic to race here. Over the years this has been the place where every land-speed record, from 300mph to 600mph, has been broken. In the 1960s and 1970s amazing jet-powered vehicles such as Blue Flame entered the record books, and drew huge crowds to watch.

Perhaps the most obvious virtue of Boneville, apart from its flatness, is that the vehicles have plenty of room to stop in this empty plain. Speed trials are scheduled throughout the summer months. In the winter, the surface becomes unstable, and the salty water is lethal for vehicle electronics.

The best time to visit is during the Bonneville Nationals Inc (BNI) annual Speed Week in August. Then you can watch the races, and meet the drivers and support teams who congregate here from all over the world. Technically, anyone can enter a vehicle, provided they've signed up for membership and their vehicle passes muster at inspection stage. This means you see vintage roadsters, Japanese rocket bikes, and just about every permutation of road vehicle in between, pounding down the salt flats.

To avoid frying, you must cover up with long sleeves and pants, and bring a hat and sunglasses (the dazzling glare from the white salt can do permanent damage to your retinas), as well as plenty to drink. But the reward for standing around in one of the most extreme settings on the planet is to watch a racing event that looks like something from *Mad Max*—and maybe even see a record or two get broken.

WHERE TO GET INTO TRAINING

While Bonneville is an awesome sight, it's nothing compared to Bolivia's Salar de Uyuni, the world's largest salt flat. Located in the south-west of the country, and covering an area of around 4,000 square miles (10,000 sq km), it boasts weird geological formations, geothermal springs, brine-filled lakes, and a vast, white salt desert. No racing goes on here (although trips by four-wheel drive are increasingly popular), but it is a working landscape for salt production, and the bitter tang of sodium chloride is in everything. You can even spend the night in a salt hotel built out of blocks of the stuff, and containing carved salt furniture.

Find Hotel California

The Eagles' seminal track from the album of the same name inspired a whole raft of rumors as well as questions. The truth is you can visit the hotel—and check out anytime you like—as long as you can afford the room rates.

"Hotel California" captured the hedonistic spirit of the mid-1970s, and teenagers around the world could recite its lyrics by heart—and wonder collectively what on earth they meant. There were rumors that it was about a lunatic asylum, and claims that a ghost inhabited the eerie cover. Some even said the song was a work of Satanist propaganda. Most of all, people wanted to track down the place immortalized in the song.

Truth is rarely as exciting as myth, and the building on the cover is the exclusive Beverly Hills Hotel photographed from an unusual angle. To capture the hotel's pink-domed roof behind a line of palm trees, the cover's creators David Alexander and John Kosh are supposed to have stood on a cherry picker on Sunset Boulevard waiting for the sun to go down. The motley crew inside the album cover were not photographed at the Beverly Hills but in the lobby of Lido Hotel at 6500 Yucca Street, LA—a building now converted into private apartments.

One side-benefit of the search for Hotel California is that over the years an establishment by that name in Todos Santos, Mexico has attracted a steady stream of pilgrims looking for pink champagne and ceiling mirrors. While this pleasant small hotel in Baja California offers plenty of luxuries, it isn't in any way connected to the lyrics.

Experience life behind bars

With its cramped cells and spectacular views over San Francisco Bay, Alcatraz Island is an unforgettable experience made all the more poignant by the participation of former inmates.

It's undeniably chilling to leave the bustle of Fisherman's Wharf behind, and take the short ferry journey to the Rock. Its situation in the inhospitable waters of San Francisco Bay makes it virtually impregnable, and it's easy to imagine how bleak the future must have looked to arriving prisoners.

Although there were plenty of escape attempts, Alcatraz only "mislaid" three of its inmates during its 29 years as a penitentiary. To this day no one knows if the three men immortalized in the film *Escape from Alcatraz* survived the journey to shore on their home-made raft, but the million-dollar reward remains unclaimed. The prison closed in 1963, and after being abandoned to the elements and then occupied by protesting Native Americans, the site became a National Park, and now provides a safe haven for bird and animal life.

The best way to tour the prison cells is with the aid of the cellhouse audio tour. Commentary supplied by former inmates paints a grim, and sometimes unbearably sad portrait of growing old behind bars. For many of them, one of the worst things about life on Alcatraz Island was that they could see the lights of the city and, on certain nights, hear the sounds of freedom and revelry emanating across the water to their dank prison cells.

Go hunting for pirate treasure

Tired of the routine nine-to-five of your job? If you would rather spend your time looking for pieces of eight then you could do worse than follow the trail of Captain Henry Morgan.

That old adage "dead men tell no tales" has meant that buried pirate hoards have generally stayed that way. The good news for would-be buccaneers is that gold doesn't rust and neither do precious gems disintegrate. In principle, billions of dollars of booty is just sitting there waiting to be discovered. However, since devoting a lifetime to the quest is beyond most of us, it is far easier to follow in the footsteps of a legendary burier of treasure, and Henry Morgan is probably your best bet.

Immortalized in several films as Captain Morgan or Captain Blood, this pirate died in Jamaica in 1688; unusually for one of his profession, he had become Sir Henry Morgan and passed on peacefully in his sleep. He was probably the most successful buccaneer of all times, and stories of his buried treasure are legion. He allegedly stashed some of his ill-gotten gains from the Siege of Panama in a bayou near Darien Bay (Panama). Other stories refer to booty on islands near Tenerife. An even stronger legend concerns a hoard on Old Providence Island off the coast of Nicaragua. Unfortunately, no one knows for sure where, although neighboring San Andres Island does have a Morgan's Cave. This could be a likely candidate, but one small detail you should know before you set off: Morgan's lair is said to be below the water level, and guarded by trusty pirate sharks.

FOUR MORE PIRATE HOARDS

1. CONNECTICUT SHORE Captain Kidd was a squirrel. Quantities of gold, silver, and gemstones were recovered from Gardiner's Island after he was captured. What about the rest? Numerous tales tell of caches secreted up and down the Connecticut coast and river, although they are said to be protected by ghosts.

2. BELIZE English pirates used Belize to stage raids on the Spanish Main, and it seems likely this tropical hideout is where most of that treasure is buried. Belize is possibly the only nation founded in part by pirates' wealth—surely some of it is left behind?

3. COSTA RICA Scores of expeditions have tried and failed to find treasure on "Cocos Islands." It's said Benito Bonito, a Portuguese pirate, buried his hoard here, as did the captain of the Lark. As if that wasn't enough to send you off with a shovel and compass, in 1822, some 11 boat-loads of booty, part of the Great Treasure of Lima, were secreted here by Captain Thompson of the brigantine Mary Dear.

4. OCRACOKE ISLAND Ocracoke Island Edward Teach aka Blackbeard is thought to have buried treasure in hundreds of places around the Carolinas. With up to 14 wives checking under his mattress, this probably seemed the safest option. Ocracoke Island was his headquarters when he met his end in 1718. Teach's Hole in the south of the island is a good place to start your quest.

Tour the world's most sinister prisons

Here are five more former penitentiaries that are open to tourists, and allow you to experience the dark and inhospitable conditions that prisoners of the past were subjected to as part of their punishment.

1. Cork City Gaol
From the outside it's a fine castle-like building, but its cramped cells housed prisoners bound for Australia on convict ships. It was also home to famous Fenians including author of *The Galtee Boy* John Sarsfield Casey, Countess Markievicz, and Frank O'Connor.

2. Old Melbourne Gaol
Located next to the Old Magistrates Court, this lock-up shop sent prisoners to trial—or to the gallows. You are walking in the footsteps of former inmate Ned Kelly when you look around. There are candlelit tours to make the experience more atmospheric.

3. Robben Island
South Africa's island penitentiary off Cape Town is most famous for imprisoning apartheid protestors, including former president Nelson Mandela. Now some tours of the prison are led by ex-political prisoners.

4. Tower of London
This impregnable fortress on the banks of the Thames is home to the Crown Jewels, but also the Bloody Tower and Traitors Gate. More ghoulish still are the carvings made by desperate prisoners on the walls of Beauchamp Tower.

5. Ushuaia National Prison
Argentina's Tierra del Fuego is not the most hospitable region at the best of times, but for prisoners forced to endure cold and cramped conditions, it must have been purgatory. The prison sits in the grounds of a naval base, and can be combined with a trip to the Maritime Museum.

Chase a tornado

If you want to live on the edge, join a safari on its quest to find the perfect storm. These driving vacations take you to the heart of Tornado Alley, with long hours on the road, and the promise of truly lousy weather.

SPOT A DUST DEVIL

Like tornados, dust devils occur when hot air rises and meets cooler air above it. They are most common in arid and desert regions such as the southwestern US and southern Australia. Usually they are harmless, although occasionally they can cause damage to people and property. Curiously, they have also been spotted coursing across the surface of Mars.

Tornados can happen just about anywhere, but the most storm-prone zone by far is the US, with around 1,000 every year. These violently rotating funnels may reach speeds of 300mph (480km/h), flattening everything in their path. The epicenter of this violent activity—known ominously as Tornado Alley—is the flat central belt between North Dakota and Texas, also taking in Nebraska, Kansas, and Oklahoma.

Storm-chasing is big business in the US and well-equipped crews carrying sophisticated weather forecasting kit record and monitor the storm cells for weather centers and the media. Some also take along paying vacationers.

A typical day begins with a discussion of the forecast and best "hunting ground." After that, tour groups take to the road, sometimes driving many hundreds of miles to find the big one. Most storms occur from mid-afternoon until early evening, so it can be a long day with little time for rest stops and meals. Peak hunting season usually lasts from mid-March to the end of May.

Experience an earthquake

No one wants to feel the ground move for real, but two Orlando, Florida attractions let you experience the nearest thing to it by taking scary simulator rides that measure on the Richter Scale.

Universal Studios Florida's *Earthquake: The Big One* ride is about as close as you can get to experiencing an earthquake without being in fear of your life. The simulator show uses San Francisco's Fisherman's Wharf as one of its backdrops, and during the simulated subway ride you experience what an earthquake registering 8.3 on the Richter Scale would feel like (that's bigger than the quake that destroyed San Francisco in 1906).

You hold on for dear life as underground trains crash in front of you, petrol trucks catch fire, water pipes rupture, and buildings collapse. Perhaps the most impressive thing about the ride is that it incorporates almost 650 gallons (3,000 litres) of real water—all of which gets recycled ready to scare the next bunch of willing victims.

A slightly less extreme ride (only 5.3 on the Richter Scale) is available at WonderWorks, a bizarre upside-down building at Pointe Orlando. While nowhere near as scary as the Universal Studios ride, it still shakes you with force equivalent to the 1989 San Francisco earthquake.

PREPARING FOR THE REAL THING

A simulator in The Tokyo Northern Disaster Research Center near Nishigahara subway station lets members of the public experience an earthquake as a public service. This is because Japan is one of the most earthquake-prone zones on earth, and learning how to react to a tremor is considered an essential part of disaster preparation.

Ride a famous cable car

Better than a fairground ride, cable cars are a great way to see the sights from a new perspective and get panoramic photo opportunities. Here are six of the best journeys.

1. Klein Matterhorn

This cable car starts in the Swiss village of Zermatt and takes you all the way to the top of the Matterhorn, where the air is a little thin, but the views over France and Italy are magnificent.

2. Mérida Cable Car

This epic cable-car journey in the Venezuelan city of Mérida rises to a dizzying height of 15,635ft (4,765m) in a journey of almost 8 miles (13km). The views can be amazing,as long as the fog hasn't closed in over the Andes mountains.

3. Sandia Peak Tramway

Running all the way from the north-east of Albuquerque to Sandia Peak 2.7 miles (4.3km) away, this gives views over Sierra Nevada Valley and Domingo Baca (TWA) Canyon.

4. Singapore Cable Car

This flies you from Mount Faber to the island of Sentosa, crossing Keppel Harbor along the way. If you want to be really frightened, take one of the glass-bottomed cabins.

5. Table Mountain Aerial Cableway

Not only does this historical cable car take you to the lofty heights of Table Mountain, but it gets you there in under six minutes thanks to recent renovations. On the way up you have a panoramic view of Cape Town, Table Bay, and Robben Island.

6. Teleferic de Montjuic

One of Barcelona's most popular tourist rides, this cable car flies you straight from the beach to Montjuic Castle, where you have great views across to the city and the port.

Cross a country and a continent by train

The Trans-Canada railroad is an epic coast-to-coast journey across the second-largest country in the world. With a route that runs 4,000 miles (6,400km), this takes in unforgettable scenery and classic tourist sites.

Canada's trans-continental railroad system was both a monumental engineering feat and an essential means of uniting this vast country. Today you can travel from Vancouver in British Columbia to Halifax, Nova Scotia, taking in the Canadian Rockies, the prairies, and Great Lakes. Choose a tour based around one section, or go coast-to-coast with stops at Canada's best sights along the way.

That this railroad was completed at all is amazing, considering the near bankruptcies that dogged companies engaged in opening up the West. While you stare at the amazing landscapes from your window, spare a thought for the Chinese and European navvies who had to hack and blast their way through almost impenetrable terrain. One of the most spectacular examples of engineering is the "Spiral Tunnels" at Kicking Horse Pass in British Columbia. Impossibly steep gradients meant creating curved tunnels that loop their way down the valley. It's still a thrilling ride and a technical challenge for the train driver.

The most iconic of the builders, Canadian Pacific Railway, was more than just a rail company, creating superb destinations to attract passengers. Well-heeled travelers in the 1920s might be heading to the Empress Hotel in Victoria, the Banff Springs Hotel, or the impossibly grand Château Frontenac in Quebec City. It's a treat to stop off at one of these stately hotels today—even if it's just for a cup of coffee and a circuit of the lobby.

FIVE MORE EPIC TRAIN RIDES

1. CHIHUAHUA AL PACIFICO

The route from Los Mochis to Chihuahua City crosses 39 bridges and nearly 90 tunnels and takes you from sea-level to an altitude of over 8,000ft (2,500m) before descending again. Mountains, ravines, and six canyons make this 13-hour journey unforgettable.

2. SETTLE TO CARLISLE

A shortie at only 72 miles, but this historical English railroad line takes you through the Yorkshire Dales, over the immense Ribblehead Viaduct, and into Blea Moor tunnel, before a more sedate run through Eden Valley. Steam train services are laid on for railway buffs and tourists.

3. THE GHAN

A journey through Australia's Red Center, this route runs from Adelaide, via Alice Springs, and on to Darwin. It takes 48 hours and transports you almost 1,865 miles (3,000km). The name is an abbreviation of The Afghan Express—the camel train once used to transport goods north.

4. TOKAIDO SHINKANSEN

Japan's Bullet Train is among the fastest and smoothest rides in the world, traveling at speeds of over 186 miles (300km) an hour. The original and best route is from Tokyo to Kyoto and Osaka, passing by majestic snow-capped Mount Fuji.

5. TRANS-SIBERIAN EXPRESS

A legendary journey from Moscow to Vladivostock, this crosses the Urals, and circuits Lake Baikal before heading into Siberia. These days you can take the journey as a luxury jaunt, minus the ubiquitous potato soup that sustained pre-Glasnost travelers.

Test your nerve on the world's steepest funicular

With an incline of 52° and a descent of 587ft (178m), Scenic World in Katoomba, Australia offers a heart-in-mouth ride down the side of a cliff tunnel into Blue Mountains rain forest.

Katoomba's funicular started life hauling coal for a mine in the Blue Mountains, which may explain why it's such an uncompromising descent for passengers. It is officially the world's steepest funicular, and if you don't like heights it's a good idea to avoid the seats at the front—or maybe forget the ride altogether. On your way down, you'll just have time to notice how the railroad is cut into the sandstone cliffs, before you enter a dark tunnel, and emerge on the other side into lush forest.

If that doesn't satisfy your craving for scary rides, the recently opened Skyway carries you high above the forest, giving fabulous views over Katoomba Falls, and the Blue Mountains' famous Three Sisters rock formation. The glass floor allows for an uninterrupted view of the valley 885ft (270m) below you.

A HISTORICAL MOUNTAIN RAILROAD

Steam engines began taking tourists from Llanberis Station to the top of Snowdon, the highest mountain in England and Wales, over a century ago. The rack-and-pinion railroad has an average gradient of 1 in 8, a considerable feat of engineering. Trains aren't going to Summit Station until they finish refurbishing it, but at Clogwyn 2,500ft (760m) above sea level there are great views. From here the peak is around an hour's hike, but worth it on a clear day to see all the way to County Wicklow in Ireland.

CHAPTER 4

Great Creations

Epic highways, great bridges, and soaring skyscrapers give a taste of the magnificent engineering achievements of the 19th and 20th centuries, but this chapter also looks back through time to ancient stone circles, Roman ruins, and the mythical and mystical landmarks of the landscape. We've included some of the world's finest parks and gardens alongside museums, grand houses, and curiosities, including an Indian temple on the British coast, and a fabulous folly in the Californian countryside. You will also find iconic city landmarks, famous and less well known, offering great vistas, and not-to-be-missed photo opportunities.

Visit the most southerly towns

Testimony to the pioneering spirit of early settlers who journeyed to the ends of the earth, despite appalling weather and an unpromising landscape, the world's most remote communities are in South America.

Chile and Argentina both lay claim to the most southerly town—and the winner depends on your definition of town (and the kind of nightlife you are expecting). Punta Arenas in Chile (70° south) can fairly claim to be the largest community at the end of the earth, with a population of about 120,000. To many though, Ushuaia in Argentinian Patagonia wins the prize. It's located at 67° south, and has a respectable population (around 45,000 at the last census).

Puerto Williams on Chile's Isla Navarino is a little farther south, but with a population of under 2,000. Around 1,000 tourists a year make it as far as Esperanza in the Argentinian Antarctic (which lies at 63° south), swelling its population of under 60. But it could be disqualified since it is considered a base rather than a permanent settlement.

FOUR THINGS TO DO IN THE FAR SOUTH

1. VISIT TIERRA DEL FUEGO NATIONAL PARK Take the "train to the end of the earth" from Ushuaia.

2. TAKE A TRIP IN THE BEAGLE CHANNEL Named after the ship that carried Darwin, this stretch of water is paradise for naturalists

3. WATCH THE PENGUINS Seno Otway and Magdalena Island are both good spots to watch penguins congregate.

4. GO SKIING IN JULY Cerro Mirador Ski Center offers spectacular views over the Pacific from hills west of Punta Arenas.

Experience the world's most northerly party town

Longyearbyen has just 1,700 inhabitants, but this glacier-shrouded town on the Svalbard islands in Norway's frozen north has proved that you don't need a huge crowds or a balmy climate to have a good time.

This is a place that describes itself as having a "relatively mild climate" when its average winter temperature is 7° fahrenheit (-14° celsius), and the mercury typically climbs to an average 43° fahrenheit (6° celsius) during the summer months. Located 78° north of the Equator, Longyearbyen hosts an annual Sunfest each March to celebrate the return of perpetual sunlight after more than four months when the town is in darkness. It also has two music festivals—blues to mark the beginning of polar night in October and jazz in January (presumably to keep everyone going until the sun comes up).

It has pubs, restaurants, a nightclub, and an ATM, but most visitors are there to experience wilderness. This is one of the few party towns where you can spend your days treking by dogsled or visiting ice caves. Winter visitors can forgo the town's Radisson Hotel and choose the Boat in the Ice at Tempelfjor—a frozen rather than floating hotel housed in an old Dutch schooner.

POLAR BEARS AND PARALLEL UNIVERSES

The Svalbard Islands are the location for much of the action in Philip Pullman's *His Dark Materials* novels, so fans will want to look out for a parallel universe guarded by Panserbjørne, a super-race of armored polar bears with opposable thumbs on their paws. You're far more likely, however, to see real-life polar bears—in fact you need to be extremely cautious about journeying outside the city limits unless you're in a well-prepared group.

Journey an extreme highway

You'll need to be self-sufficient and savvy to tackle the famous Gunbarrel Highway in Australia—and some knowledge of basic car mechanics could come in very handy.

This track traverses Western Australia and the Northern Territory from Wiluna to Yulara, and it is classic Outback country, only recommended for experienced trekkers in four-wheel drive vehicles. It was the first road surveyed by famous bushman Len Beadell, and is named after his Gunbarrel construction team (you'll find plaques commemorating his work along the route). The road was built to serve a weapons research facility called Woomera, built during the Cold War years.

You are advised to let the police at Wiluna know before you start your journey, and then check back on arrival at your destination, since breaking down could mean a long wait for a passing motorist. Enough water, fuel, and food supplies are essential—particularly as a 310 mile (500km) stretch beyond Carnegie Station has no fuel or food, and only the occasional borehole for emergency water supplies. Temperatures can be searingly hot during the day and cold at night, but there are stunning views of Oz's Red Center.

CAMEL TREKKING – OZ STYLE

Before the advent of motor vehicles, camels were the best means of transportation around the Australian interior, and thousands were imported for use by exploration and construction teams. Today several companies offer trekking safaris by camel—a novel way of exploring the desert, and also recapturing the spirit of those pioneers. The camels carry all the food and equipment you need, and there's no danger of breaking down. Most tours are accessed from Alice Springs and the opal mining settlement of Coober Pedy.

Drive the planet's longest highway

For sheer distance, you can't beat the Pan-American Highway linking Prudhoe Bay, Alaska, with Ushuaia in the far south of Argentina on an epic 29,800 mile (48,000km) route.

Purists may argue that the Pan-American doesn't qualify as a single highway, since on the North American side it's a network of roads that use different names—but this is still a pretty impressive route. The Pan-American signs start on the Mexican border, and then the road snakes down through Panama before coming to an abrupt halt at the Darién Gap. This 54 mile (87- km) stretch of rain forest on the Panama/ Colombia frontier is notorious for swamps and drug smugglers, making it impassable for all but the most foolhardy adventurers.

You can pick the Highway up again on the Colombian side and then it hugs the Pacific coast, working down through Ecuador, Peru, and Chile, before crossing over to Buenos Aires for the final stretch through Patagonia and Tierra del Fuego.

RECORD-BREAKING NATIONAL ROADS

The longest national highway in the Americas is the Trans-Canada, which links Victoria in British Columbia with Saint John in Novia Scotia—a distance of nearly 4,900 miles (7,900km). This used to be the longest national highway, but the opening of the last stretch of the Moscow-Vladivostok Federal Road in 2004 put it into second place. If you want to drive the 6,200-mile (10,000-km) route linking western Russia with its Pacific coastline, be prepared for potholes, bandits, and a scarcity of roadside cafes. The road was first mooted in 1966 and work on it began in 1978. The final Chita to Khabarovsk section was completed thanks to a EU loan, and a hefty chunk of Russia's road-building budget.

Visit a grand dam

The Hoover Dam was an incredible construction project. Built during the Depression, it stands as a monument to progress, and offers fabulous views and classic Art Deco architecture.

Although the Hoover Dam was built out of necessity, it is a thing of beauty and a testament to the thousands of construction workers and their families who lived in Black Canyon—or Hell's Hole as it became known—in the very early days of construction. Until they moved into Boulder City in 1932, these workers had to survive appalling shantytown conditions.

Temperatures could be freezing at night and searing during the day—so hot, in fact, that the only way to get concrete to set was to pump in refrigerated water. The most dangerous job was in the early stages of construction when loose rocks had to be removed from the canyon sides. High scalers were employed whose job it was to hang precariously from ropes, hammering the sides of the canyon away, or using dynamite where more force was required.

When you view the dam today—organized tours are a popular side trip from Las Vegas—it's worth remembering how much of the construction was done by hand. Although originally the power plant buildings were going to be utilitarian, there was a change of heart, and an LA-based British architect called Gordon Kaufmann gave them elegant Art Deco flourishes more suited to the scale and importance of the project. Today, thanks to this dam, the Colorado River irrigates over 1.5 million acres of land in the US and Mexico, generates hydro-electric power for three states, and supplies water for some 14,000,000 people.

Sail an engineering triumph

It's an unforgettable sight to watch vast liners or cargo ships navigating their way through the narrow channel of the Panama Canal. Its benefits to shipping have been huge, but construction was far from plain sailing.

The dream of an easy route from Atlantic to Pacific started as far back as the 1600s, when Spanish *conquistadores* considered constructing a canal across this narrow isthmus in Central America. The total canal length would be under 50 miles (80km) but the benefits would be huge—cutting the journey from coast to coast, and avoiding the perilous waters of Drake Passage and Cape Horn.

It took over two centuries before the idea came to fruition. A French company began construction in 1879, but from the start workers were plagued by accidents as well as appalling levels of malaria and yellow fever. Eventually the company went bankrupt, and the canal lay unfinished until the US took up the baton at the turn of the 20th century under President Roosevelt. By the time this vital shipping artery opened in 1914, it had taken 34 years and cost an estimated 30,000 lives.

Today, over 12,000 ships use this route every year, and you can cruise from coast to coast or visit for the day. You get a great vantage point from the visitor center at Miraflores Locks near Panama City, and can watch up to three vessels go through the lock at any one time. It takes around ten minutes for them to be raised 52ft (16m) if heading toward the Atlantic, or lowered if entering the Pacific. More impressive still is the view from the visitor center at Gatun on the Atlantic side where the water adjustment is some 85ft (26m) through the three locks.

Visit a temple to travel

St Pancras is among the most lavish railroad stations ever built, and a classic example of Victorian Gothic architecture. Inside its cathedral-like exterior are the remains of a deluxe hotel that broke the bank.

Railroad stations were a symbol of progress to the Victorians—but also places designed to inspire confidence. In the early days of steam engines many people believed the human body could explode at speeds of over 30mph, so architects looked to churches and cathedrals for confidence-building inspiration, literally creating temples to travel.

William Barlow designed St Pancras' lofty train shed arch, the largest enclosed space in the world when it opened in 1868. Then Sir Gilbert Scott (architect of many churches and workhouses) set to work on the façade. The arched Gothic windows, huge clock tower, and liberal use of red brick made it London's most imposing station by far.

But it was the hotel that really inspired awe. The Midland Grand was a palace when it opened in 1868—all marble and granite with fine murals, a gold-spangled ceiling above the central staircase, and gold leaf on the bedroom walls. Unfortunately, it was also a financial disaster, since too few bathrooms and too many fireplaces meant squadrons of servants (around 300), and despite the ultra-modern hydraulic lifts travelers preferred the comfort of West End establishments.

The hotel was always in the red and it closed in 1935. Over 70 years on it is being transformed again into a temple to travel—this time as the hub for Eurostar trains—and at least some of the Midland Grand ambience remains within a new five-star hotel.

FOUR MORE FABULOUS STATIONS

1. BERLIN HAUPTBAHNHOF This new building in Berlin is Europe's largest railroad station. It is a giant five-level operation, and the vast glass-and-steel construction looks most impressive when it's illuminated at night.

2. DUNEDIN STATION This 19th-century edifice reflected the New Zealand city's status as a major trading hub. While the white colonnades and granite pillars are impressive, the stained glass windows and mosaic-tiled floor inside the foyer are even more of a period piece.

3. GRAND CENTRAL STATION A ten-year legal battle was fought to save this iconic New York station. Restoration in the 1990s means you can once again enjoy the sparkling Sky Ceiling in the main concourse, and tell the time by the lustrous opal-faced clock. To recapture the glamor of train travel head for the tiled Oyster Bar.

4. STAZIONE CENTRALE Milan's monumental main station took almost 20 years to build, and was designed to impress—if not intimidate—when it opened in 1931. The architect of this classical giant was Ulisse Stacchini, and some Milanese think he overdid it, but the façade and ticket hall are awesome and it's now undergoing restoration.

Take a skyscraper tour

If you think it's amazing that skyscrapers go up and stay up today, then check out the early blueprints. Chicago was home to the first of a new style of architecture, and you can still spot building milestones today.

The skyscraper was born in Chicago, and the Windy City is justly proud of its heritage. Immense buildings define its skyline today, but they are only possible because of the ground-breaking designs that preceded them. Adding height meant finding new ways of supporting the weight of the building, and so innovative skeleton frameworks were devised. These pioneer builders took some risks, and helped to define the architecture of the 20th century and beyond. All this was done without computer-aided design, modern concrete-pouring techniques, and high-tech cranes.

Chicago Architecture Foundation runs river tours to give you a sense of the city's heritage and the best introduction to the skyline is the two-hour Historic Skyscrapers walk around downtown. You'll see the 12-story-high Rookery, the city's oldest surviving high-rise erected in 1888. You can admire the Auditorium Theater, a ground-breaking design with an innovative raft foundation to support the weight of its walls. There's also the Marquette Building, a 17-floor steel-framed design that was a huge influence on later architects. If you check out the lobby atrium you'll see a fabulous mosaic frieze designed by Tiffany.

Highlight of the tour is the Art Deco Board of Trade building, an imposing 44-story design housing the city's futures exchange, and topped with a statue of Ceres, the goddess of corn.

Visit five of the best skyscrapers

Skyscrapers define a skyline and sometimes a city. Here are five of the most celebrated tall buildings that you can admire for their architecture or ascend for their views.

1. Burj-Al-Arab

The world's tallest hotel at 1,053ft (321m), it's shaped like a tall sail and offers a fabulous free light show every evening. There are panoramic views across Dubai from the Al Muntaha restaurant. The ride up in the elevator is part of the experience.

2. Chrysler Building

It's not as tall as the Empire State Building but it is a New York icon, and many consider it the most beautiful skyscraper ever constructed. It still holds the crown for tallest brick building, and looks fabulous when the windows in its stainless steel spire are illuminated.

3. Taipei 101

This pagoda-inspired financial center in Taiwan was named 101 for the number of floors. It stands 1,671ft (509m) tall, and when it opened in 2004, it entered the record books as world's tallest building. It also has the world's fastest double-decker elevators so hold onto your hat. Indoor viewing is on the 89th floor, with an outdoor deck on the 91st.

4. Petronas Towers

These soaring twin towers clad in glittering stainless steel and glass dominate the skyline of Kuala Lumpu,r and held the world's tallest crown from 1998. They are connected by a sky bridge, which is open to visitors.

5. Jin Mao Tower

Shanghai's rapidly rising skyline offers plenty of iconic buildings, but at this 1,380ft (421m) skyscraper you can enjoy the world's highest hotel rooms or head to the observatory on the 88th floor. If you prefer a room in a more offbeat hotel, head to the Space Hotel at the sputnik-style Oriental Pearl TV Tower.

Find out what the Romans have done for us

The Romans built things to last, and there is plenty of evidence of their craft and ingenuity. Here are five examples of their legacy that we can still admire—and even use—today.

1. Town planning

Ephesus in Izmir, Turkey offers a fine example of Roman civic-mindedness. You can admire the façade of the Library of Celsius, see the town hall, and stroll through the Gate of Augustus before checking out pristine Roman public conveniences.

2. Good roads

Straight roads helped the Romans manage their empire, and you follow their trail by travelling the Appian Way in Italy (Rome to Puglia), Via Augusta in Spain (the Pyrenees to Cadiz), or Dere Street (York to Edinburgh).

3. Bathing

While it took centuries for the British natives to be persuaded of the benefits of cleanliness, the Romans were quick to utilize our natural thermal springs. In the city of Bath you can check out the remains of the Roman temple and take a dip yourself.

4. Water supply

The Romans didn't invent aqueducts, but they did create some of the most complex designs. Pont du Gard near Remoulins in the south of France is an outstanding feat of engineering and stonemasonry.

5. Sewers

Built with customary efficiency, Roman sewers are still in evidence today. Check out the Cloaca Maxima (Great Sewer) outfall at Rome's Ponte Rotto.

EXPERIENCE A ROMAN THEATER

If you want to see a show in a Roman amphitheater, head to Fiesole near Florence where the 3,000-seater Teatro Romano hosts drama, music, and dance performances every summer.

Watch the burning of a Viking longship

The Vikings are coming, every January in the Shetland Islands, with a unique local festival. The most spectacular sight at one of the world's oddest events is the ritual burning of a longship.

Up Helly Aa is a crazy name, but then this is a pretty strange festival. For one thing, it's held on the last Tuesday of January, cold in most parts of Scotland, but particularly inclement on the beautiful but breezy island of Shetland. Then there is the outlandish procession, as fully grown men dressed in full-on Viking armor and silly helmets maraud (in friendly fashion) through the streets of Lerwick dragging a replica Viking galley behind them.

These Vikings descend on schools, hospitals, and residential homes during the afternoon to ensure that everyone gets a chance to enjoy the invasion. Then in the evening the real fun begins. The torches are lit and crowds proceed through the streets before razing the galley that they have so painstakingly built for this celebration.

THE ELVES OF HAFNARFJORDUR

Iceland is Viking Central and if you head to Hafnarfjordur, close to Reykjavik you can learn more about this ancient culture. One of the main draws to the area is that it boasts the country's largest settlements of elves and dwarves. These "hidden folk" live in rocks around the town and are taken very seriously—even affecting the planning of roads and houses. You can get a map of their homes from the local tourist information office or take an organized tour. Make sure you check out the residence of the elvish royal family at Hamarinn cliff.

Tour a lost kingdom

Machu Picchu is steeped in romance. Discovered in 1911, it was initially called the "lost city," but over time many archeologists have speculated that it was actually a sanctuary for the Inca elite.

It may be Peru's "must-see" visitor experience today, but Machu Picchu still retains an air of Indiana Jones-style mystery. The remote location makes it easy to imagine how American archeologist Hiram Bingham III felt when he encountered such a mighty citadel at the top of a remote mountain.

Bingham named it the "lost city," but today it is believed Machu Picchu (Old Mountain) was a sanctuary for the elite. The only way in was along the same Inca Trail that hardy adventurers embark on today. Even if you take the soft option, and catch the tourist train to Aguas Calientes, it still feels as if you're following in the footsteps of the ancients when you see the Sun Gate.

Inside the city you can wonder at the artistry of the *ashlar* (dry stone walls), and also wonder how the rocks were hauled up the mountain side, and assembled with such skill. As well as the main sights—the Temple of the Three Windows, observatory, and the mysterious stone block described as the "hitching post to the sun"—there are the jails, houses, and elaborate remains of an irrigation system. All this points to a well-ordered city. As to the inhabitants, it's thought that they were nobility, high priests, and most importantly virgins who devoted their lives to worship of the sun god. Of the skeletons found during original excavations, almost all were women. Buried along with these human remains is the story of why Machu Picchu was abandoned—and what grisly fate befell its population.

FIVE MORE MYSTERIOUS CIVILISATIONS

1. ANGKOR, CAMBODIA

This city surrounded by vast temples (including the most famous Angkor Wat) was the capital of the Kmer kingdom from the 9th to the 15th century. At one time, this empire founded by Jayarvaman II stretched as far as the borders of Burma.

2. BORUBODOR, INDONESIA

The world's largest Buddhist temple complex stands sentinel on the hills close to the ancient Javanese sultanate of Yogyakarta. It was built by the Saliendra Dynasty and construction dates back to around 780AD.

3. GIZA, EGYPT

The last survivor of the original Seven Wonders, the pyramids at Giza are over 4,000 years old. More than a century of archeology and Egyptology has unraveled fragments of this advanced culture. Theories abound about who or what the Ancient Egyptians worshipped, and how they managed to construct such precise buildings. Some people remain convinced that the pyramids were created by aliens.

4. PETRA, JORDAN

The beautiful "rose red city" was home to the Nabateans over 2,000 years ago. These master planners chose a location on a major trade route, and built their city at the end of a narrow gorge known as the Siq. The vast complex of temples, tombs, and obelisks is all the more spectacular because they are hewn out of the rock face.

5. TEOTIHUACÁN, MEXICO

Once the largest city in the Americas, this site is packed with mysteries, including who founded it. We know that the people who lived here worshipped gods, evidenced by the Pyramid of the Sun built around 100ad. At its height, this city wielded huge influence in the region, but sometime around the 6th century it declined.

Commune with the ancients

Stonehenge is one of many ancient stone circles—some would argue it's not even the best—but it has captured the imagination of visitors down the ages, and remains steeped in folklore and mysticism.

With remains dating back to around 3000BC, although the site may have been used long before that, Stonehenge in Wiltshire has become a worldwide symbol of our ancestors.

Legends have always surrounded the site. It was linked to King Arthur, the Romans, Saxon,s and Danes before scholarly surveys in the 19th century finally concluded that this was a Bronze Age temple. To this day, there are myriad theories as to how the stones got there—a great feat since the largest weigh upward of 50 tons. Recent excavations close to the site have uncovered the largest Neolithic village ever found in Britain, leading archeologists to believe that this is where its builders lived. They also believe Stonehenge was part of a much larger complex.

At the heart of the circle lies the horseshoe arrangement of stones known as trilithons, and their significance has spawned many theories—both academic and fanciful. The assembly of partygoers, pagans, and mystics who gather here at dawn each summer solstice to watch the sun's rays pierce the central arch are in no doubt as to the temple's true meaning.

AMERICA'S ARTISTIC HENGES

Roadside America, the website archive of weird and wonderful US attractions, lists a catalog of marvels including the famous Carhenge in Alliance, Nebraska (monument of old wrecks), Stonehenge II in Kerrville, Texas (a retired oilman's folly with bonus Polynesian sculptures), and Foamhenge in Natural Bridge, Virginia (a practical and lightweight Styrofoam alternative).

See more Neolithic wonders

You don't have to journey far across Europe to find stone circles, burial mounds, and other reminders of the rituals and beliefs that shaped our ancient forbears' lives. Here are more impressive sites to visit.

1. Avebury Many visitors rate this above Stonehenge; you can visit both on the same day. It's older, larger, with huge earthworks, a giant circle, and an impressive stone avenue.

2. Carnac The wild regions of southern Brittany are home to over 3,000 mysterious monuments dating as far back as 5000BC.

3. Newgrange This Megalithic passage tomb in County Meath, Ireland is an awe-inspiring sight, particularly if you're lucky enough to be there for the winter solstice sunrise when a shaft of light streams through the roof box.

4. Skara Brae, Scotland Orkney is a Neolithic-sleuth's paradise, with standing stones, ancient tombs, and perhaps best of all, a pristine Neolithic village, complete with Flintstones-style home furnishings.

ANCIENT CAVE PAINTINGS

Stone circles and tombs remind us our ancestors could build, but cave paintings bring them to life; we see the world through their eyes. Two of the best caves are Altamira in northern Spain (which inspired Picasso's art,) and Lascaux in south-western France. Unfortunately, the carbon dioxide caused by the breath of generations of awestruck visitors has threatened their preservation. Lascaux was closed in the 1960s but you can see a reproduction at nearby Montignac. Altamira is also closed for now—its on-site museum contains a painstakingly rendered reproduction of the main chamber paintings.

Visit Europe's most spectacular new temple

Tucked away down a side street, just off one of north London's major roads stands an exotic white fairytale creation faced in 5,000 tons of glittering white marble and limestone.

The Shri Swaminarayan Mandir covers an area of 65,347sq ft (6,071sq m), and boasts seven pinnacles, six domes, and almost 200 pillars. It is not only the jewel in Neasden's crown, but one of the most lavish buildings constructed in London in the 20th century. The story of how this Hindu temple was built has something of the fairytale about it, too. It was funded entirely by donations and fundraising, including one of the largest ever can-recycling schemes.

Quarried Italian and Bulgarian marble and limestone were shipped to Kandia, India, where artisans worked around the clock to carve over 26,000 stone pieces—Hindu deities, intricate tracery workm and lavish carved columns and arches. Once individual pieces were finished, they were numbered and shipped to the UK to be assembled jigsaw-style.

It was built without the use of iron or steel frames, since steel is not in keeping with traditional architectural guidelines for Hindu temples. Instead, its frame is of timber and the wood carving inside the prayer hall is almost as magnificent as the marble-clad exterior.

When it opened in 1995, it was claimed to be the largest operational Hindu temple outside of India. In any setting, this would be an awesome sight, but in a suburb whose previous landmark building was Ikea, the furniture store, it stands out like a beacon. As well as being a place of worship, Shri Swaminarayan Mandir houses a sports hall, health center, vegetarian café, library, and museum. Visitors are welcome provided they are appropriately dressed and there are often guides available.

Explore Spain's Moorish masterpiece

Granada's most famous building, Alhambra Palace is also one of the world's great examples of Islamic architecture, and a reminder of the days when this part of southern Spain was an outpost of Mecca.

Standing on a plateau in the Sierra Nevada enclosed by fortified walls, Alhambra became the royal palace of the Nasrid Dynasty in 1238, although its strategic position meant that a stronghold had existed there for at least three centuries before that.

Spain's Islamic rulers were ousted in 1492, and successive Christian monarchs did their best to wipe out traces of Alhambra's glorious architecture, remodeling, and covering up parts of the original Nasrid Palaces, and building a Renaissance-style pile on part of the plot. Napoleon even attempted to blow the whole thing up and by the 19th century, Alhambra was in disrepair.

The fact that parts of the original have survived at all is something of a miracle—and Alhambra's success as a tourist attraction means you are advised to secure tickets to visit before you book your flight to Spain. Highlights are the intricate tiles and gilded ceiling in the Hall of the Abencerrajes, and the Oratory containing surviving fragments of text relating to the Koran. But perhaps the most memorable section of the palace is the Patio de los Leones, a secluded terrace containing a white marble fountain held aloft by 12 sculpted lions, and surrounded on all four sides by ornate colonnades.

Climb a holy work in progress

Antonio Gaudí and Barcelona are synonymous, but the modernist architect's most striking legacy to the city is the Sagrada Familia, a basilica that would not look out of place in Tolkien's Middle Earth.

This towering church with its strange pointed spires was started in 1882 and is very much a work in progress. Gaudí devoted 40 years of his life to its construction, and when asked about the slow pace of construction he joked: "The patron of this project is not in a hurry." Other architects stepped into the frame after his death, working from reconstructed plans, as many originals were destroyed during the Spanish Civil War.

The façade is incredibly detailed, with carvings of winged angels and strange animals, as well as words from the liturgy. And as you climb the narrow steps up the tower (not a journey for vertigo sufferers) you get close-up views of the carvings and can admire the way they appear to spring from the stone. On the Nativity Façade, a stone cypress tree is growing out of the spire; columns on either side of the central doorway are supported by a tortoise and a turtle.

Completion is scheduled for 2025, although sceptics think it could take at least another two decades. When it is finally finished Sagrada Familia will have 18 spires, including one standing 560ft (170m) tall. Although computer-aided design has speeded up the building, cranes look set to be a feature of the skyline around the basilica for years to come. There is no doubt of its importance as a landmark. Gaudí's original crypt and Nativity Façade have already been designated a World Heritage site by UNESCO.

Visit a ruin and a revival

Coventry Cathedral was destroyed in 1940 and the very next day a decision was made to rebuild. When the striking modern building was finally consecrated, it became a symbol of hope and unity.

Once one of Britain's finest medieval cathedrals, Coventry was destroyed during a fierce night of bombing, with only the tower spire and outer wall left standing amid the rubble. Basil Spence won the competition to design its successor, and this was built next to the ruins, left as they fell as a mark of remembrance.

Spence's design had its critics but over time it has become a cherished building, not least because the ruins were incorporated and are clearly visible through the dramatic West Screen. Leading post-war artists contributed artworks to its lofty interior. Perhaps the most beautiful is John Piper's abstract stained-glass window in jewel-like primary colors.

The most iconic objects in the new cathedral are fragments that were retrieved from the old one—two roof timbers that had fallen in the shape of a cross, and another fashioned from three medieval nails. The "Cross of Nails," as it is known has become a powerful symbol of reconciliation.

DRESDEN'S RESTORED CATHEDRAL

The destruction of Dresden in 1945 was one of the darkest hours of the war with huge losses of life—and of architecture. The building that was most missed was Frauenkirche, a Baroque masterpiece with an incredible bell-shaped dome. International donations helped finance its rebuilding, and the new cathedral was consecrated in 2005. The gold cross that tops the new dome was made by a British goldsmith whose father took part in the Allied bombing raid.

Tour the ramparts of a fairytale palace

Pena Palace in Sintra, a short ride from the Portuguese capital Lisbon, is an unbelievable confection situated on a rocky crag overlooking the Atlantic coast.

The whole town of Sintra is a delight with its medieval buildings, cobbled streets, and grand hotels. Even so, nothing quite prepares you for Pena Palace. Sitting right at the top of a steep hill, and surrounded by what feels like an enchanted forest, it is a multicolored jumble of towers, ramparts, and arches. It is considered Portugal's great contribution to Romantic architecture, and there is nothing else quite like it.

It was built in 1839 when the German husband of Queen Maria II bought the ruins of a monastery, and decided to convert it into a "small" palace. He employed a German architect Baron Eschwege, which might explain why in places the building looks distinctly Bavarian in style. But Eschwege let his imagination rip, and the architecture mixes Moorish and Gothic in with Portuguese medieval elements to create a delightful hotchpotch. Even the colors of this palace are fanciful—pinks and yellows blend with more formal dark brickwork to create something straight out of Disney.

You can tour the lavish internal rooms, including some preserved areas from the original monastery, but the best view by far is from the ramparts. As you circuit the palace's exterior walls you have spectacular and sometimes dizzying views over the plains below to the Atlantic coast, and the palace feels as if it is suspended in mid-air.

Enjoy a right royal extravagance

Brighton Pavilion started life as a coastal getaway and metamorphosed into Britain's most extraordinary palace, awash with Eastern promise, and masses of gold trimmings.

It is pure and unadulterated eccentricity, an Indian palace plonked in the center of a British seaside town, but Brighton Pavilion started life as a humble farmhouse, rented by the future George IV when he was enjoying sea air and a rest cure for his gout. At first this seemed the perfect place to escape the stuffy London court, and enjoy the company of his secret wife, Mrs Fitzherbert.

Eventually George's love of the high life got the better of him and he called in the builders. First Henry Holland extended the love nest, transforming it into what was known as Marine Pavilion. This was not what you'd call discreet, but once George became Prince Regent in 1811, he was able to let his imagination run riot. He employed architect John Nash, and by 1826 it had become a little bit of India by the seaside.

George reserved his most extreme decorating fancies for the interior. You can marvel at the music room with its lotus chandeliers and wall canvases depicting Chinese scenes. The enormous banqueting room features yet more Chinese scenes and a central light supported by an evil-looking dragon. Then there are the carved palm trees, imitation bamboo staircases, and the truly lurid Yellow Bow Rooms upstairs.

When Queen Victoria came to the throne the palace fell out of favor—it appears she was not amused by either the décor or the sea views. It was bought by Brighton in 1850 and remains the town's most celebrated piece of high camp architecture.

Visit the world's first museum

The British Museum was among the first to open its collection of antiquities for public enjoyment. It all began because one avid collector had amassed a treasure-house of objects.

Sir Hans Sloane was an inveterate collector, as well as a physician and scientist. Born in Ireland in 1660, he showed an early interest in botany and studied chemistry at Apothecaries Hall in London before touring France to learn medicine. It was during travels to Jamaica as physician to the island's governor that he began collecting and cataloguing flora and fauna. He returned home laden with copious notes and trunks full of treasures, as well as a recipe for a health tonic called milk chocolate.

By the time he died he had acquired so much stuff—books, plants, coins, antiquities, gemstones, and oddities such as a mummified finger—that his home employed a full-time curator. The collection was offered to the nation for $40,000 and the British Museum opened in Bloomsbury in 1759.

Over the next century it acquired treasures that are still on the top ten of exhibits for visitors today—the Rosetta Stone, Elgin Marbles, head of Ramesses, and sculptures from the Temple of Apollo and Halikarnassos. Sloane's vast flora and fauna collections later became the cornerstone of the Natural History Museum, which opened in South Kensington in 1881.

Early visitors had much more chance to get close to exhibits and this led to a few unfortunate incidents, notably the smashing of the priceless Portland Vase in 1845 when a drunk hurled a Persepolitan sculpture at its glass case. The vase has been painstakingly restored, but look very closely and you might spot evidence of Victorian vandalism.

See an embarrassment of riches

The Hermitage started life as a private collection for the Empress of Russia and became a vast depository of art and antiquities, ranging from the treasures of Troy to artworks by Rembrandt, Renoir, and Picasso.

The Hermitage began as a monumental buying spree for Catherine the Great's private collection, and opened its doors to the public in a purpose-built art gallery less than a century later. Today it occupies six buildings on the bank of the River Neva, including the magnificent Winter Palace.

This is not the sort of place you can do in a day—or even a month. In fact, fine-art fatigue is one of the perils of stepping through the door, so it's a good idea to go with a focus. There are 50 rooms devoted to Oriental art alone, with another 120 for Western art and sculpture. You could check out the magnificent collection of arms and armor in the Arsenal, or head straight for the Treasure Gallery to gawp at the bejeweled Dresden statuettes and priceless snuff boxes.

While you may be exhausted from your tour, you've only had access to a fraction of the three million items in the collection, which is why the Hermitage has spread its wings. You can view branches in London's Somerset House, Amsterdam's Nieuwe Kerk, and Las Vegas's Guggenheim Hermitage. A new branch is also planned for Ferrara in Italy.

GO ON A FABERGÉ EGG HUNT

Don't head to the Hermitage expecting to see the famous Fabergé eggs. Of the 20 or so remaining in Russia, most are on display at Moscow's Kremlin Armory Museum. One of the best public collections outside Russia is at Virginia Museum of Fine Arts in Richmond.

Explore Medieval treasures in New York

One of the strangest and most beautiful buildings in New York is the Cloisters, a 1930s museum designed around chapels, halls, and cloisters from medieval Europe, and filled with priceless art treasures.

One of the jewels of Manhattan is tucked away on 190th Street, offering the peace and history of old Europe in a unique 1930s building. The collection of treasures inside it spans the Romanesque and Gothic periods, and all were collected across Europe at the beginning of the 20th century. Highlights include the Unicorn Tapestries, woven in Brussels in about 1500, and a fantastic illuminated prayer book painstakingly engraved for the Duc de Berry. But the star of the show is the museum itself—a 1930s design that incorporates much more ancient buildings.

Much of the collection was amassed by sculptor and avid medievalist George Grey Barnard, and later bought by the Metropolitan Museum of Art thanks to funding from John D. Rockefeller. The problem of what to do with the larger exhibits, including 12th-century cloisters and a vaulted ceiling from Pontaut Chapter House, was solved by getting architect Charles Collens to incorporate these glorious remnants into a new design. Rockefeller bought the land where the museum stands, also donating a further sizeable acreage across the Hudson River in New Jersey to ensure the view from the museum wasn't spoiled.

It really is a place of peace and contemplation, particularly if you stroll around the Romanesque cloisters or wander through the beautiful period-style courtyard containing medicinal herbs and flowers that would have been grown in monastery gardens.

Try time travel in Glasgow

The Burrell Collection is a one-of-a-kind museum spanning ancient Rome to 19th-century Europe. Visiting this award-winning modern gallery is like taking a tour through time.

Sir William Burrell was a Glasgow magnate whose family fortune was built on shipping. While Burrell stepped up to the task of running the firm, his real passion was collecting. He began while he was still in his teens. According to the *Oxford Dictionary of National Biography,* he recalled infuriating his father by using his pocket money to buy a picture rather than a cricket bat.

By the time he presented his collection to the city of Glasgow in 1944 it ran to over 8,000 objects, ranging from fragile lace to a massive church doorway. It had long ago outgrown his home at Hutton Castle, and even after he had handed everything over, he continued adding to the treasures, typically spending at least £20,000 each year on acquisitions.

Today they stand in a purpose-built modern gallery in woodland outside Glasgow, not exactly fulfiling Burrell's request that it be 16 miles from the city to avoid air pollution, but coming close to the scenic setting he'd envisaged. Beginning in the courtyard, you pass the Warwick Vase from Hadrian's villa at Tivoli. Then it's on through the sculptures, reliefs, and bronzes of ancient Egypt, to a gallery focusing on Greece and Rome. One of the finest galleries is dedicated to Chinese art, and includes Neolithic burial urns, porcelain, and carved jade. There's a room devoted to early Islamic artefacts, a peerless collection of tapestries, and an area showcasing works by painters Degas, Cézanne, and Boudin. Even the corridor to the restaurant is lined with sumptuous medieval stained- and painted glass.

Tour the most decadent summer camp

You need time and comfy shoes to tour Hearst Castle in San Simeon. The architect's original brief was to "build a little something." The resulting estate had 61 bathrooms, 41 fireplaces, and rooms stuffed with an eclectic selection of artworks.

When newspaper tycoon William Randolph Hearst inherited the Californian ranchland where he spent many happy childhood vacations, he decided he was tired of roughing it, and commissioned architect Julia Morgan to come up with a more comfortable summer retreat. This was to become the wildest of all follies, absorbing 28 years of Hearst and Morgan's lives—and it was never finished.

You can't help but admire the audacious design incorporating all the architectural styles Hearst most admired. The main house Casa Grande is modeled on a Spanish cathedral, but inside you find a bedroom based on the Doge's Palace in Venice, a sombre Gothic study for business meetings, and a medieval-style Assembly Room with walk-in fireplace (for not-so-cosy evenings around the hearth).

In all there are 38 bedrooms in the main house, plus extras in three smaller guest-houses. Visitors used to fly into the estate's private airport, and could relax by watching movies in the specially built theater or find a quiet spot in one of 19 living rooms. There are also 127 acres of landscaped gardens filled with statues. Hearst packed the castle with artworks—from Tiffany lamps to antique ceilings and priceless Greek vases. The most luxurious spots on the estate are the two swimming pools. Neptune Pool is a giant marble-lined outdoor retreat surrounded by Greek-style colonnades and statuary. The indoor version is a sumptuous mosaic-lined replica of a Roman baths.

See London's most opulent bachelor pad

The Victorians had a reputation for stuffiness, but Lord Leighton's home is a lavish and indulgent bachelor pad, made famous by its not-so-faithful copy of a Moorish palace.

Frederic Leighton's artistic career was made when he sold a painting to Queen Victoria and he gained celebrity status, hanging out with the Pre-Raphelites, and creating a popular genre of art based on classical mythology. He also had a reputation as a great party-giver, hosting A-list events before the term was invented.

Just over a decade after he came to the queen's notice he moved into Leighton House in fashionable Holland Park, West London. Designed for him by George Aitchison, this home-cum-studio is one of the UK's most jaw-dropping examples of high Victoriana. It is also where you can find work by some of the greatest craftsmen of the era, including William de Morgan, Walter Crane, and Edgar Boehm.

The highlight is the Arab Hall, loosely based on the palace of La Zisa in Palermo. A combination of tiles collected on Leighton's travels to the Mid East is interwoven with Crane and de Morgan's interpretation of the Arab style. The effect is overwhelming—apparently several of Leighton's party guests fell into the hall's black marble fountain after a good night. Leighton was a prodigious collector, and although most of his Chinese pottery and Italian statues were sold after his death, you can still admire paintings by Millais, Burne-Jones, and Watts, as well as Leighton himself. The bright red top-floor studio where he did most of his entertaining gives a snapshot view of what it must have been like to be a guest at one of the finest artistic "salons."

Fly the world's most popular attraction

It's official—the London Eye is the world's most popular tourist attraction. It is also the city's most iconic structure. Not bad for a design dreamed up at the kitchen table.

The London Eye has gone into the record books as the world's tallest observation wheel, the highest vantage point in London, and according to buildings database Emporis, the most visited tourist attraction in the world.

This is no mean feat considering it was only erected as part of the capital's Millennium celebrations. Within months of its opening in March 2000 it was clear the Eye was a huge hit; within two years over 8 million had taken a flight 443ft (135m) above the Thames. At one point, it appeared it might have to close due to a dispute over ground rent, but by this time no one could imagine London without the Eye.

The observation wheel, the first cantilevered structure of its kind in the world, was dreamed up at the kitchen table of husband-and-wife architectural team David Marks and Julia Barfield. Having come up with a brilliant idea, they then had to realize it, a mammoth task that took over 1,700 people in five countries. Perhaps the biggest technical challenge was getting the 640-ton structure from horizontal to vertical position. Eventually, it was carried by barges along the Thames (with only inches to spare under Southwark Bridge), and raised by one of the world's tallest floating cranes.

It has 32 capsules—one for each London borough—each capable of holding 25 people. Private parties and "champagne flights" are popular, and it also hosts weddings and civil partnerships. While larger wheels are planned in Shanghai, Las Vegas, and Berlin, and Kuala Lumpur has already unveiled a half-sized version, the Eye's architects have the satisfaction of knowing they flew first.

FOUR MORE CITY ICONS TO VISIT

1. CHRIST THE REDEEMER

The 125ft (38m) figure of Jesus, arms outstretched, is one of the most potent symbols of Rio de Janeiro. It stands atop the Corcovado mountain so it appears to embrace the city below it. The most atmospheric journey to the top is via the historical rack railroad. Completed in 1931, the statue had a chapel added in 2006 to allow baptisms and weddings to take place there.

2. EIFFEL TOWER

The tallest man-made structure until the Chrysler Building carried off the crown in 1930, this 984ft (300m) tower was built by Gustave Eiffel to mark the centenary of the French Revolution in 1889. An engineering and construction feat that still draws huge crowds, it required 50 engineers, 100 ironworkers, and around 120 laborers to construct.

3. STATUE OF LIBERTY

A gift from France to the USA and designed by Gustave Eiffel (see below left) this 300ft (93m) copper and iron structure was shipped in 350 pieces and reassembled on Ellis Island over four months. Liberty's crown has seven spikes, representing the continents and seas of the world.

4. SPACE NEEDLE

Built to mark the World's Fair in 1962, this Seattle landmark stands 600ft (184m) high, and was the tallest building west of the Mississippi when it was completed. Today the Space Needle is dwarfed by the city skyline, but the viewing deck at 518ft (158m) still allows for good views of Mount Rainier and the Cascades. Appropriately, in a city famous for its caffeine intake, the original design is said to have been sketched in a coffee house.

See a monument to fallen idols

Statue Park in Budapest has got to be one of the most surreal places on the planet. Here is the last resting place of fallen idols—massive statues and reliefs of Lenin, Marx, Engels, and the Soviet Soldier.

When the Iron Curtain came down so did the statues. Former Soviet Bloc countries wasted no time destroying or defacing the symbols of their years under the Iron Fist. However, Hungary chose a more far-sighted route. It proposed that statues should be gathered up and placed in a special garden, and the Budapest General Assembly ran with the idea, holding an architectural competition to come up with a design. The park opened in South Buda in 1993, two years after the withdrawal of Russian troops.

The project had to be handled with sensitivity; while Western tourists might see this as a fabulous snapshot of another era, and even enjoy the iconography of these symbols, to Hungarian eyes they could be a painful reminder of oppression. For that reason, the park has a stated "no irony" rule, merely displaying them without comment. This doesn't stop the massed effect being surreal, especially when from some angles a giant Lenin appears to be waving encouragingly to a group of fallen heroes.

There are 42 pieces altogether, and although Hungary had many more available, the designers wanted to leave it be, freeze-framing the spirit of 1992 when the park was conceived.

While Lenin, Marx, Engels, Dimitrov, and other glorious heros of the Revolution are dotted around, Stalin is noticeable by his absence. There was only one statue to Uncle Joe in Budapest, and that was smashed to smithereens in the 1956 revolution.

Enjoy some strange icons

Statues can be of heroes, politicians, and martyrs, but the ones we love best are sometimes more whimsical. Here are celebrated meeting points, targets of thieves and vandals, and witness to countless holiday snaps.

1. Greyfriars Bobby, Edinburgh

This memorial is in honor of a Victorian Skye terrier Bobby who stood sentinel by his master's grave for 14 years—only leaving once a day for food. He was a celebrity during his lifetime, attracting crowds to the gates to see him appear at the sound of the 1 o'clock cannon. The granite statue and fountain were unveiled in 1873 opposite Greyfriars Churchyard.

2. Hatchiko, Tokyo

This small bronze outside Shibuya subway station is also dedicated to a loyal little dog. Hatchiko walked his master to the station every day and met him each evening. When his master died the dog continued waiting every day at the station for a decade. A sad story but Hatchiko's memory lives on—this is Tokyo's most famous meeting point.

3. Little Mermaid, Copenhagen

The youngest daughter of the Sea King has been immortalized in Copenhagen Harbor and has become a symbol of the city. Modeled on a dancer and financed by a brewer, she took up her rocky perch in 1913. Since then she's been knocked down, decapitated, dressed in a bra, and painted red.

3. Mannekin-Pis, Brussels

This statue is dedicated to a small boy relieving himself. No one quite understands why it was commissioned, but he was sculpted in 1619, so has acquired some gravitas. Over the centuries, he's been kidnapped by British and French armies, and become a target for students. He has a lavish selection of outfits, which are displayed at the Musée de la Ville de Bruxelles.

Hear music in The Americas' oldest opera house

Opened in 1856, Teatro Solis in Montevideo has played host to a who's who of great stars, and is a reminder that this city once rivaled Buenos Aires for glamor and wealth.

Giacomo Puccini, Enrico Caruso, Arthur Rubinstein, and Anna Pavlova have all topped the bill at Teatro Solis. Its location, in the sleepy Uruguayan capital Montevideo, makes this grand edifice all the more surprising. But the opera house reveals something of this capital's former glory, until it was eclipsed by the city of Buenos Aires, across the River Plate, Buenos.

When Teatro Solis was conceived, Uruguay was still a young country, having only broken free from Portugal (and before that Spain) in 1828. Montevideo's prosperity was built around its port, and it had close links with Europe through trade and immigration. In around 1840 a group of businessmen formed a company to finance a theater worthy of their independent capital, and commissioned first an Italian architect and then a Spaniard to create its Neo-classical exterior. No expense was spared and it features Russian red pine, European marble, and gold leaf from Genoa. The building was finally finished in 1856, and for many years was an essential venue on any music or theatrical tour of South America. The grand auditorium with its five-tiered balconies is a spectacular sight, and if you look up there's a dazzling gold ceiling with an enormous chandelier in the center.

An expensive six-year program to restore this grand old lady was completed in 2004 (two years ahead of its 150th birthday), with the theater reopening on Uruguayan Independence Day. International opera is back on the bill in Montevideo.

Tour six great opera houses

From Beijing's "egg" to Sydney's sails, here are opera houses that offer an unbeatable combination of architecture, atmosphere, as well as world-class music, and theater performances.

1. Bolshoi Theater
Famous for both music and ballet, Moscow's Bolshoi dates back to 1825. Ongoing renovation work on the main building is returning the rear façade to its former glory, and restoring the once peerless acoustics botched by previous revamps.

2. La Scala
Milan's great theater was built on the site of a church—appropriate in a country where opera is a religion. It created legends out of Verdi and Maria Callas, and big names from Toscanini to Daniel Barenboim have graced the conductor's podium.

3. National Grand Theater of China
This new arrival in Chang' An Avenue has been named "the boiled egg" by Beijing residents. The glass and titanium dome contains an opera house that seats over 2,400 people.

4. Palacio de Bellas Artes
Mexico City's opera house was built in the Italian style and took over 30 years to finish. This means that while the exterior is Art Nouveau in style, the interior is classic Art Deco.

5. Sydney Opera House
The famous sail-like forms of its roof have become the iconic image of Sydney, but the construction was mired in controversy and Danish architect Jorn Utzon was only recently reconciled with Australia. Since the 1990s, he's been helping to make the interior live up to his original design.

6. Vienna State Opera
Much of this building was destroyed in the war, although the glorious 1869 façade and foyer remain. This is hallowed musical ground, and worth the visit to hear Mozart or Strauss on home soil.

See a powerhouse of modern art

Tate Modern was fashioned inside the shell of a vast Victorian power station. This industrial plant on the Thames has become a sleek modern display space—but with one notable reminder of its working past.

Even people who don't like modern art love Tate Modern. Such is the impact of this fabulous gallery that visitors come to admire the streamlined contemporary display space and use the cafés and restaurants as meeting points. Its great achievement is that it has exceeded all expectations for visitors, attracting nearly 5 million visitors in 2006—rare for any art gallery let alone one devoted to cutting edge, sometimes controversial work.

The gallery was conceived because the Tate (now known as the Tate Britain) had run out of space for displaying its contemporary collections. Various sites were considered, and initially it was thought that the former Bankside power station was simply too vast—despite its perfect position on the banks of the Thames facing St Paul's. All this changed when director Nicholas Serota paced the building one evening to get the measure of it, and realized it offered almost exactly the same floor space as Tate Britain.

There was still a small matter of turning an industrial building into a layout that could be used as a gallery. An international architectural competition was held, and the winners Herzog & de Meuron devised a plan that would keep the integrity of Sir Giles Gilbert Scott's original exterior, but introduce light and a more human scale. Virtually every wall and floor you see inside the gallery is new (along with the huge roof light), but the architects did decide to keep the vast Turbine Hall. Stripped of the giant machines that once powered the plant, this empty five-story space that you can enter for free, feels more like a gargantuan cathedral than a gallery. With such a huge area to play with, it has become home to a program of dramatic custom-built installations, most notably *The Weather Project*, Olafur Eliasson's giant recreation of sun, sky, and clouds.

FOUR ARTISTIC QUARTERS

1. ABRAMTSEVO, RUSSIA

This colony about two hours north of Moscow had its own Arts & Crafts-style movement, and attracted artists, dramatists, and musicians including Mark Antokolski and Konstatin Stanislavsky. You can tour the houses and church designed by talented residents and set in an idyllic wooded landscape.

2. HONFLEUR, FRANCE

This picture-perfect harbor town in northern France was a magnet to Impressionist artists because of the quality of the light. You can enjoy café society and tour Musée Eugène Boudin, home to works by Monet and Raoul Dufy.

3. SALVADOR, BRAZIL

Instituto Sacatar is based on an island in Bay of All Saints just across from the city, and offers fellowships to visiting artists from around the world, giving them studio space in a stunning tropical setting so that they are free to create in beautiful surroundings.

4. SANTA FE, USA

Georgia O'Keeffe was this city's most renowned resident, but the town is still famous for its artistic leanings, with a huge number of galleries showcasing everything from Native American to experimental art.

Stroll through a topiary painting

Designed by an artist and sculptor James T. Mason and his wife Elaine, Topiary Park in downtown Columbus is a remarkably detailed recreation of a famous Seurat painting.

The topiary landscape is on the site of Old Deaf School Park, a favorite lunchtime spot for offices workers in downtown Columbus, Ohio. Mason recreated the painting *A Sunday Afternoon on the Island of la Grande Jatte*, using evergreen topiary, and it is painstakingly true to the original. You can stroll among the 54 topiary people standing with parasols, lounging on the grass, or taking a boat trip on the river. Look out for the supporting characters from the painting—three dogs, a monkey, and a cat. The largest of the figures is 12ft (3.6m) tall and in 1989 the city's park department installed a pond to represent the Seine.

The original idea started small— Elaine Mason wanted a bit of topiary in their back garden—but once the painting idea had taken shape, they knew they needed a larger plot. A sympathetic park department and willing sponsors helped the dream become a place everyone can enjoy.

THREE More unforgettable TOPIARY GARDENS

1. GREEN ANIMALS, Portsmouth, Rhode Island. Overlooking Narragansett Bay, the oldest topiary garden in the USA has 80 topiary shapes—including an elephant, a giraffe, and an ostrich.

2. LADEW GARDENS, Monkton, Maryland. A famous topiary landscape created by gardener, sportsman, and socialite Harvey S. Ladew in the 1930s. It includes classic images from the hunt.

3. LEVENS HALL, Kendal, Cumbria. A rare survivor of changing tastes in garden design, this topiary landscape was created in 1694 by Guillame Beaumont, who also worked at Versailles.

Get lost in amazing mazes

When it comes to deciding biggest and oldest, this is a record steeped in controversy, but one worthy contender for the largest design is the Peacemaze in Northern Ireland.

Designed to represent the twists and turns of the peace process, the Peacemaze was constructed with the help of people from all over the country. The maze was planted in Castlewellan Forest Park, County Down— less than an hour's drive from Belfast.

It covers an area of 2.7 acres and is planted with 6,000 yew trees. The design is modelled on the human brain, and areas to challenge visitors include Rocky Road and Rickety Bridge—both based on ideas from schoolchildren, and designed to show that patience and perseverance are required on the road to peace. Visitors are invited to ring the Peace Bell at the center of the maze when they've solved its puzzle. One unusual feature of the maze is that the hedges are kept low enough to allow visitors to communicate with each other.

It won two Guinness World Records for both the largest and the longest hedge when it was completed. The trees that make up the maze were chosen for their symbolism because the yew renews itself and can live for up to 4,000 years.

THREE MORE RECORD BREAKERS

1. DOLE PINEAPPLE GARDEN MAZE, Dole Plantation, Waikki, Hawaii. Waikki, Hawaii. Planted with over 11,000 native plants including hibiscus.

2. YORK MAZE, York. This regular summer tourist attraction uses 1.5 million plants over an area equivalent to 15 soccer pitches. Designs change every year, and after two months the maze is harvested and fed to livestock.

3. HAMPTON COURT MAZE, Hampton Court Palace, Surrey. The oldest surviving hedge maze layout, and an unusual trapezoidal shape.

Visit a classic fairground attraction

Modern theme parks may offer faster, higher, and scarier rides, but you can't beat the atmosphere of a classic fairground. One of the most famous is the Prater, a period funfair dominated by a giant Ferris wheel right in the heart of Vienna.

The Prater is Vienna's great city-center park, home to a racing track, and a former pleasure pavilion (known as the Lusthaus), it harks back to the final decades of the Hapsburg Empire.

The main draw for most visitors is the fairground, dominated by the Reisenrad Ferris wheel. It was built in 1897 to mark the half-centenary of Emperor Franz Joseph 1's reign. At the time this was considered a truly amazing attraction as George Ferris's original had only been constructed four years earlier as part of the Chicago World's Fair.

Standing 200ft (60m) tall, it offers panoramic views over the heart of the old city, and has become such a part of the urban landscape that when it burnt down in 1944, reconstruction began within a year. Riding the Reisenrad also offers the chance to relive a classic screen moment, for this is the Ferris wheel where the showdown takes place in Carol Reed's sinister 1949 thriller *The Third Man*.

FIVE MORE CLASSIC FAIRGROUNDS

1. CONEY ISLAND New York's great summer resort still attracts the crowds, and fairground aficionados rave about its period architecture. You can still ride the Cyclone, perhaps the world's most famous rollercoaster. Unfortunately, the Parachute Jump (a kind of early bungee jump) ceased operating in the 1960s, although the tower is still a local landmark.

2. BLACKPOOL PLEASURE BEACH Lancashire's thrills and spills attraction was modeled on US amusement parks, and opened in 1896. Its earliest ride, Sir Hiram Maxim's Flying Machines, is still in operation. The most famous stomach-churner of all is the wooden twin-track rollercoaster known as the Grand National.

3. KENNYWOOD PENNSYLVANIA is home to some of the oldest amusement parks in the world, and this one at West Miffin near Pittsburgh is a gem. It opened its doors in 1898, and historical rides include the Jack Rabbit rollercoaster, which makes use of a natural ravine for a vertiginous descent. You can also see an early William Dentzel merry-go-round and a classic 1930s Auto Race electric car ride for children.

4. LUNA PARK, MELBOURNE Opened in 1912, this amusement park was in part inspired by Coney Island, and its iconic Mr Moon gateway (you enter through the Man in the Moon's mouth) is heritage-registered, along with its period-piece merry-go-round. The Scenic Railway rollercoaster is as old as the park, and has great views over Port Phillip Bay.

5. TIVOLI GARDENS Copenhagen's pleasure garden dates back to 1840, and has a whole host of historical buildings, including the Pantomime Theater, and a glorious Chinese pagoda. It has an elderly (built about 1914) wooden rollercoaster that you can still ride. The Star Flyer—said to be the world's tallest fairground wheel—opened here in 2006.

Visit the ultimate city park

Urban landscapes need a 'green lung', but Vancouver has a park so vast that it would be better described as heart and soul of the city. This great space is home to ancient trees, stunning sea views, and hidden nature trails.

For many visitors Stanley Park is the ultimate city park, and the best bit of Vancouver. For a world city to have a 1,000-acre oasis at its center is unique. That this should also be such a wilderness makes it truly special. The park is set on a peninsula opposite downtown and should—by rights—have become urban sprawl, except that the city council had a more civic-minded plan.

Handed over for the use of residents and visitors, it soon became everybody's back garden. There are dancing classes on summer evenings at Ceperley Meadow, and outdoor theater at Malkin Bowl. There's work in progress at Painters' Circle and community gardens sit alongside formal rose beds and old-fashioned carpet bedding. You can lose yourself at the Lost Lagoon or rollerblade the famous sea wall. There are even safe and clean beaches for swimming and sunbathing.

Paradise it may be, but the park has weathered storms—most recently in December 2006 when devastating winds blew down 10,000 trees, laying waste to almost 100 acres of forest. The outpouring of financial and practical support has proved just how many Stanley Park fans there are. This will be a lengthy restoration project, but the park remains a great destination and the must-see heart of Vancouver.

See a garden of the future

The Alnwick Garden is a major contemporary garden, fashioned from a derelict 12-acre plot and requiring vision (and epic amounts of cash) to redefine its ancient outline into a garden for the 21st century.

Set in the grounds of Alnwick Castle, Northumberland, this once-derelict plot has become one of the most ambitious new gardens of the past century—and it's not finished. This is a plot designed to appeal to (and be accessible to) everyone—which means features that children love alongside plants their parents can enjoy.

The family-friendly centerpiece is a fabulous cascade, with 120 jets plus fountains, rills, and weirs, all capable of pumping out 7,260 gallons (33,000 liters) of water a minute. There's also the world's largest treehouse, a fantasy complex of turrets, rope bridges, and walkways high in the trees. Renowned maze-master Adrian Fisher was called in to design the bamboo labyrinth, a waist-high puzzler that rustles and shivers as you walk through it.

Serious plant-lovers can head to the ornamental garden, a formal space enclosed by crab apples, boxwood, and yew hedges and over 16,000 perfumed annuals, bulbs, and perennials. Curiosities include the Poison Garden—home to legal marijuana plants along with tobacco, belladonna, and sinister ivy tunnels—and the Serpent Garden, where children can let off steam among the water sculptures.

Since it opened in 2002, Alnwick Garden has become one of the most visited gardens in Britain. It has also cost a sum that must put it on a par with the most ambitious projects masterminded by 18th-century landscape architects. It looks set to become one of the great gardens of Europe.

CHAPTER 5

Out of this World Experiences

From the ultimate in hedonism to the strange and otherworldly, this chapter looks at one-of-a-kind travel experiences. If your taste runs to unusual hotels there are underwater lodgings, palaces on wheels, and a grand old ocean liner. Or you may prefer to be showered in rose petals, immersed in chocolate, or part of the crowd at the greatest carnival on earth.

We couldn't ignore the strange—and downright spooky—so you can explore meteorite sites, spot crop circles, or take a tour around Dracula's castle. Finally, for the truly adventurous, there are trips to Middle Earth and visits to Santa, as well as your best chance to become one of the world's first space tourists.

Take a ride up an aquarium

Elevators don't get much more impressive than the one in the AquaDom. It's encased in a giant cylindrical aquarium in the middle of the lobby of the Radisson SAS Hotel in Berlin, and offers visitors a unique journey through an underwater landscape.

The aquarium, at about 80ft (25m) high, is the largest cylindrical fish tank in the world. It employs two divers to feed the 2,500 tropical fish and wave at hotel guests. Dominating the hotel's atrium, it offers travelers, who check into the Radisson on Karl-Liebknecht-Strasse in the heart of Berlin Mitte, the unusual luxury of opting for a room overlooking the River Spree or an "ocean view."

If you're not staying there, it's still worth dropping in for a drink and a fishes' eye view in the AquaLounge.

For more marine life, head next door to Sealife, which has 30 freshwater and saltwater tanks, and is responsible for maintaining the Radisson's tropical tourist attraction.

A DIFFERENT SORT OF LAKE HOUSE

Utter Inn was designed as a B&B with a twist. The romantic gabled wooden building is marooned on a tiny barge in the middle of Lake Mälaren in Västerås, Sweden. Upstairs there's a small deck where you can sunbathe or watch the lake, but downstairs, below the waterline, is your sleeping accommodation. It contains twin beds and a table—so no luxuries or acres of space—but you do have an ever-changing canvas as the fish and the waters of the lake swirl past the windows.

Tour the world's best aquariums

The best aquariums transport you to another world. You have a chance to walk through an alien environment, and get close to some of the rarest and most beautiful creatures on our planet. Here are five of the best underwater viewing experiences.

1. Georgia Aquarium

This opened in 2005 in the state capital Atlanta, and claims to be the world's biggest, housing around 500 species including whale sharks, sea turtles, and beluga whales. The front of the striking building resembles the prow of a great ocean liner.

2. Monterey Bay Aquarium

Built on the site of an old sardine cannery, this Californian institution has successfully exhibited the first great white sharks, later released into the wild. Less imposing sea creatures also get star billing—there's a school of anchovies and an area dedicated to giant sea kelp.

3. Osaka Aquarium Kaiyukan

Japan's third-largest city has devoted its aquarium to showcasing Pacific Ocean marine life, including whale sharks, ocean sunfish, and sea lions.

4. Shedd Aquarium

The elegant classical building opened in 1930 at the heart of Chicago Museum Campus. The midwestern city wasn't perhaps the most obvious setting for an aquarium—up until the 1950s, Shedd transported both its seawater and marine life in a specially designed railroad carriage! It has stunning recreations of Caribbean and Philippine coral reefs.

5. Sydney Aquarium

With the world's largest Great Barrier Reef display (in case you don't have time to make it to the real thing), this Australian visitor attraction also has platypus, seals, and crocodiles.

Dine in an underwater restaurant

A dazzling variety of seafood is on the menu in the Maldives—especially if you dine with the fishes in a stunning and intimate restaurant located underneath the ocean.

You can't get away from the sea on the Maldives, a string of over 1,000 tropical islands in the Indian Ocean. It's already a haven for divers and snorkelers, but perhaps the most stunning venue for getting up close to marine life in comfort is Ithaa, a restaurant sited 15ft (5m) underwater with a fishes' eye view of the coral reef. It was constructed by the Hilton resort, Rangali Island, and the restaurant dome is built of clear acrylic, giving diners a 270-degree view. It is one of the few chances humans get to experience what life feels like inside the aquarium—an unnerving experience when the sharks and rays decide to swim up close to eyeball your grilled lobster.

The construction, based on similar technology to the shark tunnels built through aquariums, was designed in New Zealand, constructed in Singapore, and shipped over 2,000 miles (3,220km) to its underworld home. It only has room for 14 diners, but there's plenty of atmosphere provided by the turquoise waters around it.

HAPPY HOUR IN THE DEEP

A sand floor, octopus-shaped chairs, pillars fashioned like sea cucumbers, and giant Plexiglas windows offering a panorama of the reef make cocktails in the Red Sea Star a surreal experience. This underwater watering hole 15ft (5m) below is at the end of a long jetty in the Israeli resort of Eilat. The star-shaped design means almost every guest is afforded a window seat, and the views are particularly impressive after dark.

Experience "Twenty Thousand Leagues Under the Sea"

You don't go as deep as Jules Verne's classic sci-fi novel, but Jules Undersea Lodge is an underwater motel in Florida where you can spend the night in the company of manatees and fishes.

The Lodge is a comfortable two-bedroom underwater research station 21ft (6.4m) below Key Largo's Emerald Lagoon that also takes paying guests. You can take a hot shower, watch a movie (*The Abyss* or *The Deep* perhaps?) and dine on seafood cooked by the resident "mer chef." While the setting isn't lavish, it is unique, and the real entertainment is provided by the the large viewing windows.

This protected mangrove environment is home to nurse sharks, grouper, and parrot fish as well as the occasional sea horse, puffer fish, or manatee. While you have to dive to get to your hotel, no prior experience is necessary as the staff can give you a three-hour course to ensure you can make it to and from your room in safety. Luggage and dinner are transported in special waterproof cases. There are plenty of opportunities to dive (the main draw) as well as visit the nearby research lab, and find out how aquanauts undertake research around the lagoon.

BOOK YOUR PLACE AT THE ULTIMATE UNDERWATER RESORT

When it opens in 2009, Poseidon Underwater Resort will be the world's first luxury underwater hotel. It is accessed by elevator and sits around 40ft (12m) underwater in a beautiful Fijian lagoon. Guests don't need to worry about their tans; trips combine time below with days on the beach at a private island. Start saving now because an all-inclusive week for two will cost around $30,000.

Stay at a floating palace

The Lake Palace in Udaipur must be among the most romantic and celebrated hotels in the world and its unique setting on Lake Pichola seems worlds away from the bustle of modern India.

This lavish white marble building was constructed as a summer palace by the emperor Maharana Jagat Singh II in 1746. He chose a prime piece of real estate on an island surrounded by the cooling waters of the lake, and overlooked by the Aravalli Hills. The palace covers pretty much all of the four-acre plot so that it looks as if it is floating on water.

Its reincarnation as a luxury hotel suits it admirably, and guests who can tear themselves away from their suites (sunken baths, flat-screen TVs, etc) can dine in splendid isolation on a pontoon overlooking the water, swim in the hotel pool surrounded by ornate marble pillars, or take a private boat-trip around the lake.

Back on the mainland Udaipur's lakefront is lined by an array of grand buildings including the Maharana's even more spectacular main residence, the City Palace. Don't miss the Crystal Gallery in the Fateh Prakash Palace (part of the City Palace compound and now a hotel). This is a room entirely decked out with crystal furniture—including beds and sofas—all complemented by a jewel-studded carpet. The combined effect of all this glitter can be somewhat dazzling so you might want to go armed with a pair of sunglasses.

Step back in time on a luxury liner

Queen Mary is an iconic ship, once the epitome of luxurious travel across the Atlantic, and now a treasured monument in California where you can board for the night to recapture the glamor of the 1930s.

It was an inspired move on the part of Long Beach, California to grant *Queen Mary* her final dock on the waterside in 1967. Not only has this stately liner, which was built on the Clyde, become a favored tourist attraction, but she is one of the most unique hotels in the world.

The ship was a record-breaker from the moment she slid down the launch. Cruising at 28.5 knot,s she held the Blue Riband for 14 years for the fastest North-Atlantic crossing, and during the 1930s the rich and famous graced her decks. During wartime she was painted grey, renamed *The Grey Ghost* and saw active service—carrying over 760,000 military personnel and covering almost 570,000 miles (918,000km). She finished the job after the war by carrying GI brides and children to the USA. No wonder she is classed as family by many Americans—especially those who crossed with her during service, and are honored on the Grey Ghost Wall of Heroes.

Not only is *Queen Mary* a popular venue for conferences, weddings, and parties, but you can take a behind-the-scenes tour and then drink cocktails in the Observation Bar, originally the first-class lounge. If you want to stay the night, you will be transported back in time, as the wood-panelled staterooms have carefully restored Art Deco features and original artwork.

Journey on the Orient Express

Glamor, espionage, even murder. It all adds up to one of the most romantic train routes in the world. Saved from the scrapheap by an enterprising American, this luxury train offers routes round Europe.

In the heyday of train travel there were no fewer than three Orient Express companies running a variety of routes to the glamorous hotspots (and political hotbeds) of Europe. A well-heeled traveler could board at London or Paris, and then head to the mountains of Switzerland, the olive groves of Athens, or the canals of Venice. The travel was comfortable, the food was legendary, and the company was guaranteed to be interesting.

Thanks to Agatha Christie's novel, the most celebrated route is London to Istanbul (Constantinople), as traveled by Belgian detective Hercule Poirot in *Murder on the Orient Express*. A book containing shady characters from across the four corners of Europe and beyond, it perfectly captured the sense of adventure—and a frisson of danger—of international train travel in those inter-war years.

While Venice-Simplon-Orient Express uses historic coaches and runs many of the same routes as the originals, you are more likely to be sitting next to a rail buff or lover of luxury than a murder suspect. However, the service and the destinations remain just as glamorous.

ON THE TRAIL OF AGATHA CHRISTIE

If you are following in the footsteps of Hercule Poirot, and decide to take the journey to Istanbul, make sure you stay in the Pera Palace. This grand old hotel was built expressly for passengers on the Orient Express and Agatha Christie is reputed to have dreamed up her most famous whodunit in Room 411

Sleep in the world's wackiest hotels

Hotel accommodation can be just a bed for the night, or it can define your whole trip. From underground caves to a giant crane, here are six unforgettable lodgings around the globe that give you an insight into the culture – and offbeat style – of the country you're visiting.

1. Club Hotel Casapueblo, Punta Ballena

A museum, hotel, and must-see lookout point for visitors to the nearby resort of Punta del Este, this Uruguayan creation looks like something from *Star Wars*, although some visitors say it's as close as you get to living the Gaudí dream. Created out of adobe, the extraordinary rock-like structure clambers up the hilltop and creates perfect photo opportunities, particularly at sunset. It was designed by Uruguayan painter Carlos Paez Vilaró as a sculpture you could live in.

2. Commune by the Great Wall, Beijing

Designed by 12 Asian architects and originally exhibited at Venice's Architecture Biennale, the Commune is a striking series of contemporary buildings set in wooded landscape with views over part of the Great Wall. You can stay in Airport, a crazy terminal-style design, or enjoy a more Zen-like experience in Bamboo Wall with its stunning vistas and bamboo screens. Other options include Split House, which has a brook running under the glass floor.

3. Crane Hotel, Harlingen

About an hour's drive from Amsterdam, this head-in-the-clouds retreat for two is a far cry from the windmills and canals of the tourist trail. It's fashioned from a former industrial crane overlooking the docks. Accommodation is inside the old machine room, and breakfast is sent up to you by elevator. The crane still works (the biggest draw for many visitors), and you can operate it from the driver's cabin, making the platform spin around at your pleasure.

4. Desert Cave Hotel, Coober Pedy

Extreme heat and dust have made the opal-mining town of Coober Pedy famous for its dugout lifestyle. The best way to experience this troglodyte existence is to stay at Desert Cave Hotel. It was created in the 1980s using opal mining machinery to gouge out the sandstone, and create 19 underground suites with high ceilings and natural temperature control—unlike the rooms above ground where the air conditioning is forced to work overtime.

5. Quinta Real, Zacatecas

The colonial city of Zacatecas in central Mexico has plenty of stunning architecture, thanks to its silver-mining heritage, but the views at Quinta Real are about as good as it gets. This former bullring has been painstakingly restored and all 49 luxury rooms overlook the central arena, now an impressive Andalusian-style cobbled garden. The hotel looks particularly atmospheric after dark

when the elegant colonnades surrounding the ring are illuminated.

6. Wigwam Motel, Holbrook

This wacky Arizona lodging boasts 15 teepees containing double beds, bathrooms, air con, and other essentials for modern life. They were created in the 1950s (originally part of a chain) and are now on the National Register of Historic Places. Their location—sandwiched between Route 66 and the railroad track—gives you the authentic motel experience, despite the faux Native American styling.

Travel like a Maharajah

The ultimate deluxe rail journey around India, the Palace on Wheels, gives you the chance to travel around the sights of the north in state, just like the Maharajas and Maharanis of old.

Modern travel has more associations with the cattle truck than glamor, so the Palace on Wheels is pure hedonism if you want to see the sights of India's golden triangle from the comfort of a well-padded armchair. This nostalgic slice of the life once lived by princes and heads of state is pulled by a steam engine (heaven for railroad buffs), and its 14 carriages have period wood-paneled bedrooms with the occasional modern touch such as TV, hot water, and air conditioning. Guests can choose from two restaurants with guaranteed scenic views, or chill out in the on-board living rooms.

This unique train service runs from New Delhi, and its usual seven-day route takes in the pink city of Jaipur, the mighty Thar Desert, and Ranthambhor National Park, as well as Jodhpur, Uidapur, and the Taj Mahal at Agra (see page 189).

ENJOY A JOURNEY THROUGH THE HEART OF AFRICA

Rovos Rail was founded by a group of passionate railway enthusiasts who rescued and restored vintage train coaches, attached them to lovingly maintained steam engines and created a luxurious way to see the spectacular scenery of South Africa. You can choose from two day trips along the Old Karoo Pioneering Trail between Pretoria and Cape Town or take a variety of longer journeys, including one to Victoria Falls. Rovos Air offers another five-star experience, sightseeing on classic aircraft such as the Convair 440.

Party at the best fiesta

Rio de Janeiro's legendary carnival has the best show-stopping costumes, hugest street parties, and most decadent balls, making it an essential date in the fiesta-lovers' calendar.

Carnival is the other national sport in Brazil, and visitors to the world's biggest street party in Rio during February (the four days before Ash Wednesday) can see the city's samba schools perform in the purpose-built Sambodromo. With seating for more than 70,000, this stadium offers a ringside seat on the main parade, and if you can't get tickets the atmosphere around the stadium is just as feverish.

Beyond the main parade there are organized and spontaneous dances around the city's streets, most notably in Cinelândia Square, plus parties in bars and clubs. While the dress code on the streets is scanty, there are more formal black-tie balls, including the famous star-studded gala at the five-star Copacabana Palace Hotel. Tickets to this A-listers event don't come cheap—anything from $400 to more than $1,200 a head.

HEAD NORTH TO BAHIA'S GREATEST BASH

Rio is celebrated the world over, but the whole of Brazil is feverish with the party spirit in February, and one of the greatest street parties takes place in Salvador de Bahia, the country's former capital, and its most African city. Here you can listen to fabulous music, and join in six days' of parades along 15 miles (24km) of streets—circuiting some of the most historic parts of this 450-year-old city. One benefit of this fiesta is that for now, at least, it is less overwhelmed with tourists than the Rio Carnival.

Move to a unique temporary city

Black Rock City exists for just eight days every year, and this weird and wonderful festival in the middle of one of the USA's most inhospitable and remote regions centers around the burning of a giant image of a man.

Burning Man is a festival where self-expression and self-reliance are king. The participants make the art and create the city over eight days at the end of August. The location is Black Rock Desert, Nevada, about two hours from Reno—one of the most inhospitable environments you can imagine. At 4,000ft (1,220m) above sea level, this is a flat hardpan devoid of natural shelter and subject to extremes. By day, the temperature can top 100° farenheit (37° celsius), and at night it can be sweater-and-wooly-hat weather. There are also frequent high winds and the occasional downpour to contend with. Visitors are advised to take face masks and goggles to cope with the inevitable dust storms.

Still, crowds of 35,000 or more descend on this desert, bringing everything they need to survive the eight days ahead and have some fun. That includes food, water (lots of it), shelter, sun cream, and warm clothes. When the festival ends they pack up every last shred of evidence that they were there and leave the desert as they found it.

There are strict rules governing this temporary metropolis, but it's a far cry from your average downtown. To begin with, no cars are allowed to drive round the city's playa. There is also nothing for sale at the event except ice and coffee (proceeds donated to the local town), and hawking of any description means banishment from the festival.

What is nurtured is self-expression. People are encouraged to be existentialist, exhibitionist, or whatever else they feel like in the name of art. They decorate their tents and themselves, and are urged to go create—be it a painting, a circus performance, or a giant installation. Some of them create theme camps or "villages" dedicated to special interests—from aliens and alternative healing, to Barbie and *Star Wars*.

The main event at Burning Man is, of course, the pyrotechnics. Special burning platforms allow people to burn their artworks, and fire eaters and performers entertain the crowds after dark. The most dramatic moment by far comes on the sixth day of the festival when an effigy as tall as a seven-story building is torched in front of the assembled crowds.

Enjoy other great world carnivals

You can party your way around the globe if you head to these top destinations for carnivalistas. Here are five of the best places to live it large. Just remember to pack your maracas.

1. New Orleans Mardi Gras
Undaunted by Hurricane Katrina, the party capital of the South hosts its giant parade every February. The organizing societies, known as "krewes," create fantastical floats while an alternative and more risqué party goes on in the French Quarter.

2. Notting Hill Carnival
The streets of West London host one of the loudest events in Europe over August Bank Holiday. It attracts acts from as far afield as Brazil, and draws in up to 2 million revelers.

3. Sydney Mardi Gras
This gay and lesbian carnival is fun for all, not least because of the outrageously camp costumes, and the amazing parade. It goes on for a month through February and includes art, film, and vaudeville, plus a huge party at multiple locations to round things off.

4. Tenerife Carnival
This Spanish island claims its party to mark the start of Lent is second only to Rio and, while the weather might not be so balmy, the costumes are nearly as wild. The parade in Santa Cruz is the main draw, but more offbeat is the "Burial of the Sardine" to mark carnival's passing.

5. Trinidad & Tobago Carnival
The largest pre-Lent party in the Caribbean is famous for its Mas revelers, and its seductive calypso and steel-pan musicians. Most of the action takes place in the Trinidadian capital Port-of-Spain, but the infectious party atmosphere spills out around the island.

Shop till you drop at the mega malls

Paradise or purgatory depending on your attitude to shopping, the world's super-sized shopping malls make destinations in themselves. Some are big enough to while away an entire vacation.

Although the USA invented the shopping mall, these days it doesn't even figure in the top five. The biggest by a long shot (although it may soon be dwarfed) is the South China Mall at Dongguan in China's Guandong province. It covers 9.6 million sq ft (660,000sq m), and has 1,500 stores plus a spa, nightclub, two five-star hotels, and a theme park on the site. Its motto is "where East meets West," and shopping streets include Champs Elysée, Venice Square, California Beach, and Amsterdam Street. Number two in the league is Jin Yuan in Beijing, affectionately known by resident Westerners as the "Great Mall of China."

If you want to pay homage at the biggest shopping mall in North America (fourth biggest in the world) head to West Edmonton Mall, which describes itself as Alberta's number one tourist attraction—something organizers of the Calgary Stampede or visitors to the Canadian Rockies might dispute! It has a mere 800 stores but does also boast amusement areas, hotel, indoor pool, and a staggering 20,000 parking spaces.

Surprisingly the USA's biggest shopping center only ranks 10th in the world league. Officially, it is the King of Prussia Mall in Philadelphia—although this could be disqualified, since it is technically three adjacent malls managed as a single unit.

Bargain at the world's biggest weekend market

Canny bargain hunters and tourists alike flock to Jatujak (Chatuchak) weekend market in Bangkok—almost universally regarded as the world's biggest and best street market.

JJ, as it's commonly known in Thailand only emerges in its true splendor on weekends, but when the traders flock in it covers an area of 35 acres, and is home to at least 9,000 stalls. A mobile phone and a map are a good idea as it's easy to get lost in the maze-like network of streets (the clock tower in the center of the market is the best meeting point).

You can find almost anything you want at its myriad stalls, from antiques, handicrafts, and fabrics to street food and perfect copies of designer brands. You will also be able to buy some cheap luggage to transport all your goodies home with you.

SHOP AROUND THE CLOCK AT EUROPE'S FINEST FLEA MARKET

Braderie de Lille takes place annually on the first weekend in September and draws over 10,000 traders. Not only have you got a huge number of stalls, but you can shop continuously from 3am on Saturday to midnight on Sunday. The center of the city is closed to traffic, and anyone can set up a stall to flog their wares. In the best flea-market tradition you can find just about anything—including an awful lot of what can only be classified as junk, but that's all part of the fun. Shoppers and bystanders keep their energy levels up by snacking on moules-frites (mussels and chips). Traditionally, everyone leaves their empty mussel shells in a pile by the stall when they've finished and restaurateurs compete to amass the biggest mussel shell mountain.

Be immersed in chocolate

Now this sounds like heaven on earth. You can fulfil that long-held *Charlie and The Chocolate Factory* fantasy by checking into Hershey, USA for a glamorous or gluttonous time.

This Pennsylvania town founded by Milton S. Hershey is said to be built on chocolate, and these days it's a hugely popular visitor destination—whether or not you have a sweet tooth—as it has the giant Hersheypark funfair, plus a championship golf course. Naturally it also offers the works for chocoholics—with a generous helping of whipped cream if you want it. There are train rides around Chocolate Town, tours of a simulated chocolate factory, plus endless sampling and shopping opportunities.

The ultimate indulgence though is to check yourself into the spa at Hotel Hershey for an afternoon of beauty treatments. These include immersion in a whipped cocoa bath, body scrub with chocolate-bean polish, or a soothing and tantalizingly fragrant cocoa massage.

VISIT MORE CHOCOLATE FANTASIES

1. CADBURY' WORLD, Birmingham, UK. Perhaps not the most glamorous location, but Birmingham does contain a massive visitor center at Bournville dedicated to the nation's favorite chocolate.

2. CAILLER CHOCOLATE FACTORY, Broc, Switzerland. Enjoy a thoroughly state-of-the-art tour, and of course, plenty of sampling opportunities, around this olde-worlde Swiss chocolate factory.

3. MUSEUM OF COCOA AND CHOCOLATE, Brussels, Belgium. Created by a third-generation chocolatier Mme J. Draps, this historical building close to the Grand Place offers insights into the history of chocolate, plus daily demos, and sampling sessions.

Enjoy a shower of roses

The ultimate in rose-tinted experiences happens in the Bulgarian town of Kazanlak each summer when they celebrate the region's most fragrant and luxurious cash crop.

Rose oil (attar of roses) has been prized for centuries, and Bulgaria's Rose Valley is the perfect location for growing the Damask roses used in perfume-making. The city is located in the center of the country, and surrounding mountain ranges provide the perfect combination of shelter, sunshine, and rainfall.

This crop not only looks sumptuous and smells marvelous, but it costs three times more than gold. Not so surprising when you consider that it takes 1,300 rose blossoms to make just one gram of precious oil. The roses are picked by hand in early morning, and then distilled almost immediately in copper vats to maximize their fragrance. More than 2,000 locals are involved in plucking them from the rose bushes around the town in a harvest that lasts around 20 days.

The best time to see this romantic industry at work is during Kazanlak's Festival of Roses in early June. It includes a parade, and a crowning of Queen Rose, as well as the chance to watch the picking of the blooms.

VISIT THE WORLD'S PERFUME CAPITAL

Much of the rose oil harvested in Bulgaria finds its way to Grasse, a medieval town on France's Côte d'Azur. You can tour the Fragonard, Molinard, and Galimard perfume factories, and see the perfume essences that are used by the world's leading perfume makers. Or visit Grasse's perfume museum on Place du Cours to find out about the history of scent.

View a monument to love

With its white marble facing and exquisite inlaid calligraphy, the Taj Mahal has got to be one the most romantic places on the planet. The legend behind it is a reminder of the lasting power of love.

The Taj Mahal at Agra is the most important part of the Golden Triangle tour for many visitors to northern India. Familiar the world over in photographs and film, it is still a breathtaking sight with its domes, minarets and exquisite inlaid details. Its history is shrouded in mystery, but the most orthodox account is that the temple was built by Mughal ruler Shah Jahan as a mausoleum for his wife Mumtaz Mahal, who died in childbirth.

The extraordinary monument, completed in 1648, took 17 years to build and employed over 15,000 construction workers, including some of the leading Islamic architects of the period. The cost of this shrine was staggering as it used not only the finest white marble but quantities of semi-precious stones to decorate the flower patterns inside and outside the mausoleum.

It stands raised on a platform and framed by minarets inside a formal walled garden. Built on Islamic geometric lines to represent the garden as an earthly paradise, this landscape is dominated by a central canal that focuses the eye and reflects the tomb, making this a particularly beautiful spot at dawn or dusk when the building's outline takes on a rosy glow.

Shah Jehan's remains lie inside the Taj Mahal, close to his wife and many of the interior rooms have been sealed off since that time. All this adds to the air of secrecy surrounding the complex, but for romantics this site is the ultimate testimony to love's endurance.

Visit more romantic hotspots

If the Taj Mahal doesn't awaken your romantic yearnings, here are four more destinations that have become famous as places where even the cynical and hard-hearted find it hard to escape the tugging at their heart strings.

1. Casa di Giulietta, Verona

Juliet's House in Via Cappello is a shrine for tourists on the trail of Romeo and Juliet. It has a balcony and a statue of the fair maiden outside—her right breast rubbed shiny by generations who have touched her for luck in love.

2. Casa Guidi, Florence

Elizabeth Barratt wasn't your typical runaway bride, being 41, and in poor health, but this apartment in Palazzo Guidi in Florence (one of the world's great romantic cities), became a haven for the Victorian poet and her even-more-famous husband Robert Browning. They married secretly in London, and spent 14 happy years here. You can tour the house from April to November.

3. Gretna Green

Geography put this place on the wedding map. As the first village north of the border where couples could legally marry using the Scottish handfasting ceremony, it was the scene of countless dashes by carriage and on horseback to escape pursuing guardians. To this day over 4,000 couples plight their troth here each year, and it does have a distinct "love conquers all" aura about it.

4. Las Vegas

The casinos are not the only beacon offered by Vegas. This is a wedding capital, thanks to its history of liberal marriage requirements (no waiting, no blood test). The "quickie" wedding is alive and well with a choice of chapels, and themes ranging from old-fashioned romantic to those with an Elvis accompaniment. Many people also come here to renew their vows—which is heartening.

Find a classic American diner

Before mass-produced fast food, there was the diner—the all-American place for a burger, hot dog, and fries, or a deliciously calorific milkshake. Happy days! Here are six fabulous nostalgia trips.

1. 11th Street Diner, Miami Beach
An oasis on 1065 Washington Avenue, this late 1940s design was shipped down to the warmer south from Pennsylvania, and its iconic interior has made it a popular movie location. It serves excellent mudslides.

2. Empire Diner, New York
Situated on 10th Avenue and 22nd Street, this building dates back to the 1940s, and is topped with a miniature Empire State Building. Fashionable with the Chelsea crowd, it has outdoor seating in summer.

3. Fog City Diner, San Francisco
Chilled oysters and red curry mussel stew may be on the menu alongside pastrami sandwiches, but this is still a great re-creation of the classic diner interior. It's located on Battery Street.

4. Mickey's Dining Car, St Paul
A Minnesota institution since 1937, this railroad-style design is on West 9th Street, and its Art Deco neon sign draws architecture buffs as well as hungry locals and tourists. It is a protected building and stays open around the clock.

5. Miss Bellows Falls Diner, Bellows Falls
This classic Vermont eatery appears on the US National Register of Historic Places. It was built in the 1920s and started life in Massachusetts, before heading north. Homemade cheesecake and pies are a specialty.

6. Trolley Car Diner, Philadelphia
A glorious authentic 1950s diner housed on the site of a former Roy Rogers restaurant at 7619 Germantown Avenue. You'll find hot dogs, pretzels, and ice cream on the huge menu, plus T-shirts to prove you've eaten here.

Drink famous cocktails at source

The ultimate cocktail aficionados' tour is to drink the most famous tipples in the place where they were invented. Here's a top-six of drinks to order on their glamorous home turf.

1. Black Russian

Legend has it that this vodka and coffee liqueur combo was created in the Cold War years in honor of the US ambassador to Luxembourg and socialite Pearl Mesta. The place to drink this in her honor would be the lavish five-star Metropole in the center of Brussels where it was first mixed. Try the 19ème Bar for authentic period glamor.

2. Buck's Fizz

This simple champagne and orange juice pick-me-up was almost certainly invented in Buck's in London's West End, but since this is a private member's club, it might be more in keeping with the spirit of the Roaring '20s if you drink the decadent tipple in Le Touquet. The creator of Jeeves and Wooster, P.G. Wodehouse is among the famous past residents of this resort in northern France so

where better to drink a toast than the bar of the true blue Westminster Hotel?

3. Daiquiri

Forget your fruity and frozen hybrids, the original recipe developed in Cuba is a mix of white rum, lime juice, sugar, and shaved ice. Probably the best location to sample it is Floridita in Havana. Try the equally glamorous Soho, London branch if you can't justify the airfare to the Caribbean.

4. Margarita

This lethal combination of tequila, triple sec, and lime juice is usually served with a salt-encrusted rim around the glass. At least four people claim to have been first to mix it, but one of the more likely candidates came from Baja California, just over the Mexican border. You could do worse than pick the Beach Comber bar at Rosarito Beach Hotel on Rosarito Beach. It has a long and distinguished history (Lana Turner and Rita Hayworth were once visitors), and great views over the Pacific.

5. Singapore Sling

Said to be invented around 1910, this is the only drink to order at its birthplace, the Long Bar of Raffles Hotel, Singapore. It's a heady mix of ingredients, including gin, cherry brandy, Cointreau, Benedictine, and pineapple juice. As guardians of the magical recipe, the hotel management keeps the original formula in the hotel safe.

6. Vodka Martini

Shaken and not stirred James-Bond style, this powerful vodka and vermouth aperitif may seriously impair undercover espionage work. The secret agent first drank it in the first *Casino Royale*, and since this is a work of fiction, you could mirror the plot, and pick a smart casino in the south of France—perhaps Casino Croisette in Cannes. However, the original inspiration for Ian Fleming's plot is said to be the Casino Estoril near Lisbon, Portugal.

Stop for afternoon tea

The most ancient and hallowed of rituals, indulged in from China to the UK. Although the accompaniments may vary, it is a wonderful way to while away the afternoon, and recapture the spirit of a more stately age.

1. Bettys
A Yorkshire institution serving delectable confections from its own bakery. The original tea shop is in Harrogate. Skip lunch so you can do justice to the groaning cake trolley.

2. Brasileira, Lisbon
The Portuguese are café addicts, and this Art Deco building on Rua Garrett in Chiado has long been a haunt of writers and intellectuals. It is a good stopping off point after a strenuous shopping session—don't forget to order a custard tart with your tea.

3. Café Central, Vienna
Situated on Herrengasse, this elegant watering hole is hugely popular. Coffee is Vienna's more famous drink, but tea is also on the menu, along with apple strudel, sacher torte, and other sweet pastries and cakes. Piano music serenades you in the afternoon.

4. Lak Yu Tea House, Hong Kong
A period piece in the Central District of Hong Kong, this famous tea house on Stanley Street opened in the 1930s. It's a top spot to sample green tea, and also to try the dim sum if you can find a table.

5. Willow Tea Rooms, Glasgow
Famed for its décor created by Glasgow artist Charles Rennie Mackintosh (who designed everything down to the teaspoons), this café on Sauchiehall Street serves afternoon tea all day. A popular meeting place, it's a good idea to reserve a table.

6. Windamere Hotel, Darjeeling
A revered Edwardian hotel on Observatory Hill, this overlooks the famous tea-planting town and the Himalayas. Take afternoon tea on the terrace, if you can.

Straddle two continents

Air travel has deprived us of one of the ultimate "been-there, done-that" moments. Here are three land routes that allow you to savor the moment of having a foot in two continents.

1. Bosphorus Strait

This narrow stretch of water in Istanbul marks the dividing line between Europe and Asia. The easiest way to straddle two continents is to stand in the middle of the mighty Bosphorus Bridge. A more atmospheric and old-fashioned experience is to take a cruise along the river. You can zig-zag between Europe and Asia visiting mosques, museums, and traditional fishing villages.

2. Bridge of the Americas

An impossibly romantic name, Puenta de las Americas was originally known as Thatcher Ferry Bridge—not half imposing enough for its location. It crosses the Panama Canal on the Pacific side and if you stand in the middle, you can claim you are officially between North and South America. Newer Centennial Bridge gives you the same experience but doesn't have the same history.

3. Straits of Gibraltar

This narrow gap divides Europe from North Africa and until a proposed road tunnel links Punta Palomas in Spain with Punta Malabata in Morocco, your best cross-continental experience is the fast ferry ride from Algeciras to Tangier. Around 30 minutes from the Tangier docks you should be in African waters.

DRIVE ACROSS THE ARCTIC CIRCLE

You can cross into Arctic territory if you take Canada's Dempster Highway. This great road trip is from Dawson City in the Yukon, to Inuvik in the Northwest Territories. The stretch that earns you your Arctic Circle badge is around 20 miles (32km) north of Eagle Plains.

Drink a toast to great artists

Dublin is home to some choice pubs, where both the Guinness and the literary muse have always flowed freely. Perhaps the most famous is Davy Byrnes in Duke Street.

Davy Byrnes is not just a pub, it's a hallowed part of literary history. This city-center watering hole is mentioned as being frequented by Leopold Bloom, hero of James Joyce's *Ulysses*. You can even dine on his favorite lunchtime gorgonzola sandwich with accompanying glass of burgundy (although you may prefer the seafood specialties it is renowned for these days). While Joyce is perhaps the most celebrated author who drank here, it was also a favorite stopping off place for his literary buddies, including Oliver St. John Gogarty, and James Stephens.

If that's not enough to give it entry into the literary hall of fame, legendary drinker and writer Brendan Behan was also a frequent visitor and is reputed to have had a brawl outside the pub. His father-in-law painted the murals behind the bar.

The décor is unusual for such an old pub—a bit of a 1930s time warp—but that's all part of its charm, and there are regular Joycean events held here. The biggest date in its diary is June 16 (the day the action in *Ulysses* takes place), when locals and tourists flock to the pub to honor what they now call Bloomsday by drinking a toast or three to the author.

FIVE MORE WATERING HOLES WITH LITERARY LEANINGS

1. THE ALGONQUIN HOTEL, New York. This hotel in the theater district is hallowed ground because of its long associations with Dorothy Parker and the Round Table literary group (they preferred to be known as the Vicious Circle). Their favorite spot for liquid lunches was the Rose Room.

2. THE DOVE, London. This historical pub on the banks of the Thames at Hammersmith is notable for its tiny bar packed with huge crowds of drinkers, but Graham Greene is said to have enjoyed a pint here in quieter days. Earlier still, Scottish poet and playwright James Thomson lodged in rooms above the pub.

3. BAR HEMINGWAY, Paris. This bar at the Ritz was renamed in honor of one of its most famous patrons (also see right), and F. Scott Fitzgerald also frequented its plush seats and ordered a cocktail or two. Original black-and-white photographs by Hemingway line the walls.

4. MILNE'S BAR, Edinburgh. Known as the poet's pub, this popular bar on Hanover Street in the Old Town is celebrated on Edinburgh literary tours as a favourite meeting place of the Scottish writers' scene, including Hugh MacDiarmid.

5. SLOPPY JOE'S, Key West. Hemingway appears to have seen more than a few bars in his time but Sloppy Joe's in Duval Street is one of the most laid-back. The bar honors the man in an unusual way with its annual Hemingway Look-Alike competition each July— a hotly contested international championship for anyone blessed with a white beard and authentic Papa attitude.

See the world in a day

The World has to be one of the most ambitious tourist developments on the planet. A group of 300 man-made islands off the coast of Dubai grouped like the seven continents, it is already visible from space.

Traveling from Ireland to Australia should be a breeze once the World is finished—you will be able to do it in an evening, possibly taking in Rio and Tokyo along the way. This group of islands is being constructed two and a half miles (4km) off the coast of Dubai, so one thing you can guarantee is that the weather in London will always be sunny, and you won't have to worry about scarf and mittens in Moscow, or monsoons in Mumbai.

The smallest island is just over 250,000sq ft (23,000 sq m), the largest around four times that, and prices started at under $7million—not bad considering buyers have been allowed to build what they want, and become ruler of a private paradise in the sun. Many of the smaller atolls have been snapped up by the rich and famous—interestingly, some have chosen to go patriotic and move to the island of their birth. Others will be the locations of themed resorts, including a replica Greek island, and a tropical Thai resort. One of the best places to stay will be Oqyana, based on Oceania, and including a massive shore front, linked walkways across 19 islands, and a marina with space for 1,500 private yachts. Guests will be able to bunk down in exclusive hotels, sea-view apartments, or canal boats.

Marvel at a giant meteorite crater

While meteor strikes may be the stuff of Hollywood disaster movies to most of us, they do happen. In fact, they have already changed the course of history. See the evidence at Vredefort Dome.

Formed over 2,000 million years ago, Vredefort Dome in South Africa is the oldest, largest, and most deeply eroded meteorite strike site we know about. It is estimated that the celestial body that caused this giant dent in the earth's surface was at least six miles wide, although some speculate that it could have been 25 times that size. An alternative theory says the object that hit the earth was a smaller comet that struck at such speed it created this massive geological disturbance.

Whichever theory is right, scientists are certain that this was a planet-wide event, triggering devastating after-effects. The site is easily accessible, being only about 60 miles (100km) south-west of Johannesburg; and the evidence is spread over a huge area in a series of outcrops ("koppies"). Taken together, these form a series of rings radiating out from the impact site, an almost unique feature on our planet. The Vredefort Dome became a World Heritage site in 2005, and you can hike or mountain bike around the crater or kayak along the Vaal River.

VISIT THE MOST PHOTOGENIC METEOR SITE

You can only get the true measure of Vredefort's vast size from the air. So if you are looking for a classic photo opportunity visit Barringer, near Flagstaff, Arizona. The world's first confirmed meteorite crater, this almost perfectly circular cavern with a rim of boulders around it looks like something dreamed up by a Hollywood special-effects department.

Discover more space craters

Here are locations that were shaped by the impact of a giant celestial body millions of years ago. Some have only been confirmed as impact sites recently, suggesting that many more are yet to be discovered.

1. Acraman, Australia

This remote area in southern Australia is popular with birdwatchers and bush campers, but scientists have also been drawn here to research its ancient history. A hexagonal dry salt lake lies in the center of an impact zone estimated to be at least 56 miles (95km) in circumference. Fragments (known as shatter cones) ejected by the impact have been discovered 280 miles (450km) away.

2. Chesapeake Bay, US

This Atlantic estuary is famous for its scenery, and the mighty Chesapeake Bay Bridge. But a huge extra-terrestrial object landed here around 35,000,000 years ago, creating a crater almost a mile deep. It was discovered under sediment by oil drilling in the 1990s.

3. Chicxulub Crater, Mexico

It is a beach paradise today, but buried beneath the Yucatan Peninsula is a massive geological find that may have caused the demise of the dinosaurs. Fragments of rock found in Haiti, and mining surveys of the Yucatan have unearthed evidence of a catastrophic impact around 60 million years ago that caused tsunamis, dust clouds, and mass extinctions.

4. Sudbury, Canada

This Ontario city's destiny was shaped by an asteroid over a billion years ago. The object was at least six miles (10km) across and the force of the landing cracked the earth's crust, exposing the Sudbury Basin, a valley with rich seams of nickel, copper, and platinum. Find out more at the Science North visitor attraction.

Have a close encounter of an alien kind

There are absolutely no guarantees that you'll see a UFO, let alone be victim of an alien abduction, or body probe, but there are hotspots where it is most certainly worth keeping your eyes peeled.

1. Bonnybridge, Scotland

A report in the *Scotsman* newspaper in 2005 highlighted this town's extra-terrestrial links. It is part of the "Falkirk Triangle," an area stretching from Stirling to Fife where there are an average of 300 recorded UFO sightings a year.

2. Molekba, Russia

Dubbed the M-Zone by skywatchers, this remote village in the Urals about 600 miles (1,000km) east of Moscow is the epicenter for UFO activity in Russia, with reports of numerous orbs and flashing objects in the sky, as well as sightings of strange beings in the forests.

3. Nullarbor Plain, Australia

Once used as a nuclear-testing ground, this remote treeless plain in southern Australia is a famous wilderness road trip, but also has a reputation for eerie sightings. The most famous in 1988 involved a car being apparently sucked up by a UFO.

4. Texas Triangle

The road between Texas and New Mexico is probably the most famous hotspot in the world, thanks to the Roswell Incident in 1947, when an alien craft (or research balloon if you believe official accounts) was recovered near a New Mexico ranch. This single incident sparked a frenzy of interest in alien beings.

5. Warminster, Wiltshire

Perhaps its proximity to Stonehenge has fueled the stories, but this area became a popular place for alien-watching during the 1960s. Many reports mention glowing orange balls and strange noises. Watchers still gather at Cley Hill, an Iron Age hill fort above the town.

Hunt for crop circles

Some say crop circles are a sign of alien life. Others see them as a kooky underground art form. Whatever you think, your best hunting ground is the rolling fields of south-west England in late summer.

In the late 1970s images of crop circles began appearing on the front pages of British newspapers. These mysterious areas of flattened corn or wheat appeared like strange symbols when viewed from the air. There was much speculation about how they had been made, and soon they were joining the realms of UFOs and other unexplained mysteries.

Eventually, after numerous circles and endless international newspaper reports, two Hampshire-based artists, Doug Bower and Dave Chorley, owned up to an elaborate hoax that started after an evening in the pub. It worked so well that over the next 12 years they continued to create bizarre shapes under cover of darkness. Today other "croppies" carry on their work and so the mystery is solved.

Or is it? The incredibly complex Milk Hill formation that appeared in 1981 on a cornfield above Alton Barnes, Wiltshire is considered by many to be more than human hands are capable of in a single night.

SEE GIANT WHITE HORSES

Wiltshire is also famous for its white horses—giant outlines carved in the ground exposing the chalk layer beneath. You can see examples at Cherhill, Westbury, and Alton Barnes. Most created in the early 19th century, but the Uffington White Horse, a 375ft (110m) long shape near Uffington Castle, Oxfordshire, is at least 3,000 years old. Local lore has it that this animal outline is actually a dragon.

Tour a city of the dead

Havana's Necropolis Cristobel Colon gives you a fascinating glimpse into Cuba's past. Grand mausoleums and statues to the departed line its wide avenues, creating one of the most atmospheric sights of the city.

Cuba's famous "city of the dead" in the suburb of Vedado is simply huge, covering an area of almost 148 acres (60 hectares). It's like a snapshot of the country's pre-Castro history, spanning Spanish colonial rule, and the prosperous years that followed for a privileged elite after independence. The cemetery was designed by a Spanish architect, and you can see the European influence from the moment you walk through the imposing Northern Portico. Four wide avenues criss-cross the graveyard, all leading to the beautiful Central Chapel.

It is the artistry that is most impressive. You also see changing tastes in design—from soulful-eyed angels and chubby cherubs, through to the severe black granite of Art Deco mausoleums. There are memorials to many of Cuba's most famous figures, although the country's greatest 20th-century hero, Che Guevara, lies entombed in Santa Clara 166 miles (270km) east of the capital.

For Cubans, the most important shrine in Colon is the marble statue *La Milagrosa* (the Miraculous One). It is dedicated to Amelia Goyri de Adot who died in childbirth along with her child, who was buried at her feet. Legend has it that when the body of Amelia was exhumed some years later it remained intact, and the child was now lying in her arms. The statue is easy to spot as it is usually surrounded by flowers.

Find a living god

India has had a long tradition of holy men, from swamis to full blown "God Men;" and between five and eight million people (around half a percent of India's population) claim some element of divinity even today.

Normally male, these spiritual souls generally live alone, spending their days in contemplation or Yoga. Others perform magic rituals and meditate to increase their spiritual powers, or to acquire mystical knowledge. Normally, a Hindu has to live many lifetimes to become enlightened or holy, but fast tracks are available to the devout, and on any trip to India you are likely to spot these *sadhus* (holy men). Often you may see them dressed in simple white loin-cloths close to temples or other sacred sites.

Modern cosmopolitan Indian society retains time-honored codes to support holy men. People give donations as offerings to the gods and get blessings in return; it takes a brave person even in the cynical West to deny divinity when someone is pursuing such a devotional path. The reputation and idolization of some self-styled "God Men" has spread. Raghavendra Swami and Sai Baba are worshipped all over the world, and Sai Baba is viewed by his huge following as a living and breathing god.

Although recent laws have been passed in India to curb their influence, gurus are still being courted by politicians for endorsements, especially in a holy man's home state where pronouncements may hold considerable sway. While the vast majority live devoutly and humbly, a few swamis have amassed considerable fortunes from their preaching.

THREE MORE LIVING DEITIES

1. DALAI LAMA

The most famous and revered of all living deities is the 14th in a line of Tibetan God Kings that stretches back 600 years. He has become a world symbol of peace since ascending the Lion Throne in Lhasa at the age of four, and now lives in exile with the Central Tibetan Administration, and many fellow Tibetans in Dharamsala, northern India.

2. HRH PRINCE PHILIP

The Yaohnanen of Vanuatu in the South Pacific have a legend of a spiritual ancestor who left in search of a bride. It goes on to say how he ended up in England and married a queen. That narrows it down!

Prince Philip is well aware of the reverence in which he is held by the islanders, and is reported to have discreetly sent photographs of himself holding the nal-nal (traditional war club) presented to him by the islanders.

3. SUN MYUNG MOON

Rev. Moon is believed by his followers to be the Messiah on a mission to complete Jesus' work. He heads the Unification Church, which was founded in Korea, and has since spread around the world. By 1995, he and his wife claimed to have given God's marriage blessing to 360,000 couples.

Visit five world famous graveyards

Here are five places where you can pay your respects at graves of the brave or famous, enjoy tranquility, or experience a spooky atmosphere so authentic it has featured in horror movies.

1, Highgate Cemetery
This North London cemetery is so creepy it was a film set for a Hammer House of Horror. There are persistent urban myths surrounding the Highgate Vampire, but most visitors come to see the Circle of Lebanon and Egyptian Avenue, or pay their respects at the tomb of Karl Marx.

2. La Recoleta
Buenos Aires' exclusive burial address is the place to see the grave of former first lady Eva Perón. Lavish mausoleums and memorials are jam-packed along its avenues, and the sight of so much white marble can be dazzling. Some much-needed shade is to be found under the giant Gran Gomero rubber tree opposite the cemetery gates.

3. Père Lachaise
One of Paris's most unusual visitor attractions is in a wooded setting in the 20th arrondissement. Many come to visit the grave of Jim Morrison, but you can also see the last resting places of Oscar Wilde, Richard Wright, Edith Piaf, and Frédéric Chopin.

4. Port Arthur
Tasmania's infamous penal colony gives a taste of conditions endured by prisoners, some as young as nine, in a "model prison." The unmarked paupers' graves on the adjacent Isle of the Dead are in stark contrast to the elaborate stones carved by prisoners for the free population.

5. Tyne Cot
This burial ground near Passchendaele, Belgium, for the dead of World War I is a poignant site with its row upon row of simple white gravestones. It is the largest cemetery for Commonwealth forces and includes a memorial to the missing soldiers.

Tour Dracula's castles

With its forbidding domes and turrets, Bran Castle in Transylvania has all the right credentials for Dracula's lair, although if you want to follow the bloody trail of the vampire there are two other spooky castles you should also visit.

With its hilltop position, dank dungeons, and general air of remoteness, Bran Castle near Brasov, Transylvania, certainly looks like the kind of place a vampire might favor. Its greatest claim to fame is that Vlad the Impaler was here once, possibly as a guest or a prisoner. Dracula's author Bram Stoker is thought to have used this fortress as inspiration for his classic spine-chiller. This is good enough to attract hordes of tourists and, since the castle has been used as a location for several films, it has *bona fide* star quality, too. Serious vampire-followers might also wish to check out Poienari Castle in the neighboring county of Wallachia. This hilltop ruin was one of Vlad's favorite fortresses. He must have appreciated its strategic clifftop position on the road between the state capitals of Sibiu and Pitesti.

However, there is another castle in another country that could have stronger links to the legend. Vlad may have impaled his enemies, but it seems unlikely he drank their blood. However, the infamous "Bloody Countess," a Hungarian noblewoman called Elizabeth Báthory is reputed to have murdered scores, maybe hundreds of maidens in ways too grisly to mention. She was eventually walled into Cachtice Castle, outside Cachtice village in the west of Slovakia. The castle is a ruin today, but no one has forgotten its most terrifying resident more than three centuries ago.

See more fabulous fortresses

Europe is awash with castles, from fairytale gems to forbidding fortresses. Here are five where you can soak up the atmosphere, hear about long-lost battles, and ghostly happenings, or even stay the night.

1. Castel Sant'Angelo

Commissioned by the Emperor Hadrian as a family tomb, this circular building stands sentinel over the Tiber on the route into Rome. It has been a fortress, a prison, and a refuge. Now it's a museum complete with mortuary chamber.

2. Kilkea Castle

Less than an hour's drive from Dublin, this imposing 12th-century fortress in County Kildare has its own ghost in the grounds called Gerald. An evil-eye stone at the back of the castle wards off enemies, but paying guests are welcome as this is now a fine country house hotel.

3. Kronborg Castle

Denmark's most famous castle was the setting for Hamlet's Elsinore, and sits on the edge of Zealand guarding the coast from invaders. You are unlikely to see the ghost of Ophelia, but can tour the catacombs and admire the statue of Ogier the Dane.

4. Schloss Neuschwanstein

The ultimate Bavarian fairytale palace, this castle in Schwangau, Germany, was built by Ludwig II and his romantic medieval yearnings are revealed in the abundance of heraldic images. It has an awesome Byzantine-style throne room.

5. Stirling Castle

This is Braveheart country, for William Wallace defeated the English at Stirling Bridge in 1297, and Robert the Bruce did the same at Bannockburn less than 20 years later. It sits atop a volcanic crag, and is reputed to be haunted by at least one ghostly soldier.

Enter Middle Earth

Creating Middle Earth should have been the toughest of all jobs for the set designers of *Lord of the Rings*, but New Zealand's natural assets did much of the hard work for them. Journey here to find everything from the green sward of the Shire to evil Mount Doom.

After the release of Peter Jackson's epic *Lord of the Rings* trilogy, the New Zealand tourist board could afford to put its feet up for a while. This has to be the first time a country has become one vast film set, but then it does have a uniquely varied geology. In an area slightly smaller than Italy, you can choose from soaring mountains, neat pastures, lush forests, and vast plains.

At Matamata on the North Island of New Zealand, part of the set of Bilbo and Frodo's home village Hobbiton remains, looking for all the world like a greener and pleasanter version of England. Head beyond Hamilton to Port Waikato for the forbidding slopes of Weathertop. The winter playground at Mount Ruapehu (also see page 37) became Mount Doom.

It's the South Island where the odyssey truly begins. Near Christchurch, the Canterbury Plains area and Mount Sunday became home of the city of Edoras and Court of Meduseld. Around Glenorchy and Arrowtown, a spectacular series of lakes and peaks were used to recreate landscapes of Middle Earth. Twizel in the Mackenzie Country was the natural setting for the visually stunning battle of Pelennor Fields.

There are more than enough maps and guides for visitors to rent a car and embark on a quest to find the Ring for themselves. However, it is worth taking a helicopter or balloon tour to see the full glory of the landscape around Kahurangi National Park, Mount Sunday, and Queenstown.

Explore four more out-of-this world locations

Here are earthly locations used to create either fantasy landscapes, or the world of the future. Don't expect to recognize them instantly, like all great pretenders, trick lighting and make-up were involved.

1. Batman

The first Tim Burton film created Gotham City at Pinewood Studio, but England was handy for many of the gloomy and forbidding interiors. Wayne Manor's exterior was Knebworth in Hertfordshire (better known for its annual rock festival). The interior was shot at nearby Hatfield House.

2. Blade Runner

Ridley Scott's rendering of the classic Philip K. Dick novel shows just what special effects can do. The dark and dank Los Angeles of the future was, wait for it, sunny LA. Notable buildings used as sets include the Spanish-style Union Station, and the Frank Lloyd Wright-designed Ennis House which became Deckard's (Harrison Ford's) apartment.

3. Harry Potter

It is pure wizardry the way J.K. Rowling's imagined landscape came to life. Filming for the movies has zig-zagged around Britain. Hogwarts is a patchwork of interiors including Gloucester Cathedral, Durham Cathedral, Oxford's Bodleian Library, and Alnwick Castle in Northumberland (also see page 169).

4. Star Wars

The deserts and dunes of Tunisia needed very little work to be transformed into Tatooine. In fact, there's something of a tourist trail to Onk Jamel where the desert-pod race took place in *The Phantom Menace*. You can see Luke Skywalker's home town at Matmata, the site of amazing troglodyte Berber dwellings.

Stay in an ice hotel

The ultimate winter wonderland, an ice hotel is an igloo on a grand scale, and a place where it's cool to don long-johns and a wooly hat, before you hop into your sleeping bag. Take a buddy; it's romantic and you need the body warmth.

The original ice hotel opened in the Swedish village of Jukkasjärvi, north of the Arctic Circle. A tourist company wanted to inject some fun into the dark winters, so built Arctic Hall to serve as a gallery for visiting artists. It attracted crowds, and eventually a group of hardy souls decided to rough it in the igloo for the night. They returned raving about their sub-zero sleeping quarters, and so the concept was born.

These days you can choose from standard cold accommodation in a thermal sleeping bag—still a pretty amazing experience—or pick a deluxe private suite decorated with fabulous ice sculptures and reindeer skins. If you are more worried about maximizing body heat than romance, book a communal bed to sleep four adults comfortably. In the morning, guests can hop into a sauna to warm up before heading out on a snowmobile in search of adventure.

QUEBEC'S SENSATIONAL ICE FEST

While Sweden's ice hotel is as cosy as a sub-zero setting can be, Quebec City's ice hotel gets more lavish every year, with artists going for broke to create a monument in the snow. You can dance the night away in the N'Ice Club, or sip something chilled in the Ice Lounge. Outdoor tubs are part of the experience, and the hotel even has its own chapel to marry ice kings and queens.

Meet Santa and his helpers

Santa welcomes guests each December, provided you journey all the way to Lapland. Here you can meet the man, the elves, and the reindeer—even Scrooges will find their frozen hearts melting the snow.

Santa magically appears in several Lapland locations each December, and who could deny his existence faced with such concrete evidence. You can choose from resorts such as Olos and Salla, or wilder settings above the tree line. At some locations you can reject the cosy centrally heated chalet, and ask his little helpers to build you an igloo.

Most tours include tobogganing and elf playmates for the children, while adults may want to cut up the ice on snowmobiles and skis, or try husky-mushing. Tours last anything from one to five days, and if you are taking children, it's usually a requirement to get them to write a letter to the bearded one before arrival.

FIVE MAGICAL CHRISTMAS MARKETS

1. AUGSBURG
This Bavarian city has hosted a Yuletide market for at least 500 years.

2. COPENHAGEN
Tivoli Gardens are transformed into something straight out of a fairytale.

3. KRAKOW
Traditional Polish decorations, as well as stalls selling mulled wine and sausages.

4. PRAGUE
Nativity figures, huge tree, and endless fairy lights—like a scene from a Christmas card.

5. VIENNA
The trees around the market are illuminated from mid-November. Schönbrunn Castle also hosts a gorgeous Christmas village.

Get off this Earth

If this planet just isn't exciting enough for you (and I hope this book has proved it is), there is another option. Soon it may be possible to slip our gravitational ties, and enjoy the ultimate travel adventure.

The Russian space program has been selling spaces on the International Space Station for years. Unfortunately, at $20 million a ticket and a three-year waiting list means it's not for everyone. But there are other options. At least 20 private companies are actively planning various enterprises from sub-orbital hops to fully fledged moon trips. Rockets range from garden-shed creations to far more sophisticated options, so remember *caveat emptor!*

Likely winners of this space race include Virgin Galactic, now taking bookings, and with a launch vehicle already in production. A refundable deposit of only $20,000 will guarantee you a place, giving you a few years to save.

The *VS2 Enterprise* will be one of five spaceships taking two pilots and six paying passengers. Virgin plans to take 500 guests in the first year of operations, planned for 2009. If this happens it will be equivalent to the total number of astronauts to date through national space programs. Cruising speed will be 12,000 mph (19,300km/h), and you will spend 15 minutes in space.

If for some obscure reason you don't like the idea of being strapped to a grain silo full of high explosives, but you do like the idea of wearing a shiny astronaut suit, head to Star City near Moscow for astronaut training, using real equipment for a fraction of the price of heading into orbit.

Perhaps one day we will all be astro tourists.

Useful travel links

Here is a guide to some of the most useful websites and travel links – perfect if you want to plan a journey or see what the world has in store for you.

Useful background

BBC –
http://news.bbc.co.uk/1/hi/country_profiles/default.stm

CIA World Factbook –
www.cia.gov/cia/publications/factbook

Google Earth – www.earth.google.com

National Geographic –
www.nationalgeographic.com

Travel health – www.mdtravelhealth.com

UNESCO World Heritage Sites –
www.unesco.org

Wikipedia – www.wikipedia.org

WWF – www.panda.org

Trip planners and reviews

About – www.about.com/travel

Bugbog – www.bugbog.com

Cadogan Guides –
www.cadoganguides.com

Fodors – www.fodors.com

Forbes Traveler –
www.forbestraveler.com

Frommer's – www.frommers.com

Lonely Planet – www.lonelyplanet.com

Rough Guide – www.roughguide.com

STA Travel – www.statravel.com

Time Out – www.timeout.com

Travel Channel –
http://travel.discovery.com

Travelers Digest –
www.travelersdigest.com

Trip Advisor – www.tripadvisor.co.uk

Wikitravel – www.wikitravel.org

Sights and destinations

AUSTRALIA

Australian Heritage Places –
www.heritage.gov.au

Australian National Parks –
www.australiannationalparks.com

CANADA

Canadian Register of Historic Places –
www.historicplaces.ca

Parks Canada – www.pc.gc.ca

IRELAND

Heritage Ireland –
www.heritageireland.ie

Northern Ireland
www.geographia.com/northernireland

NEW ZEALAND
National parks –
www.nationalparks.org.nz
Historic places Trust –
www.historic.org.nz

SOUTH AFRICA
National Parks – www.sanparks.org
Heritage sights – www.rebirth.co.za

UK
National Trust –
www.nationaltrust.org.uk
English Heritage –
www.english-heritage.org.uk
Scottish Natural Heritage –
www.snh.org.uk
Historic Scotland –
www.historic-scotland.gov.uk

Undiscovered Scotland –
www.undiscoveredscotland.co.uk

US
National Parks – www.nps.gov
National Register of Historic Places –
www.cr.nps.gov/nr/

Special interest
Buildings – www.landmarktrust.org.uk
New/landmark buildings Database –
www.emporis.com/en
www.greatbuildings.com
www.skyscrapers.com
Extreme sports –
www.doctordanger.com
Roadside America –
www.dinercity.com
www.roadsideamerica.com
Skiing – www.ifyouski.com
Volcanoes – http://volcano.und.edu
Waterfalls – www.world-waterfalls.com

Acknowedgements

Special thanks to John Keay for his input and ideas throughout the project, and to Robert Johnston and Nick Norman for offering up so many brilliant leads. My thanks also to Graham Potter, Karl Stanley, Robin Stewart and Simon Wotton.

Books

AA City Pack Brussels & Bruges, AA Explorer Cuba, AA Explorer Vietnam, The Book of General Ignorance (Faber and Faber Ltd), Eyewitness Travel Guides New York, Insight Guides South America, Insight Pocket Guide Istanbul, Lonely Planet Central America on a Shoestring, Lonely Planet Mexico, Lonely Planet Puerto Rico, The Rough Guide to Belize, The Rough Guide to Scotland, The Rough Guide to South America, The Rough Guide to Tunisia, Time Out Buenos Aires, Time Out Havana & the best of Cuba.

Website Resources

www.about.com, www.aboutvienna.org, www.alnwickgarden.com, www.architecture.org, www.australianexplorer.com, www.australianfauna.com, www.baldeagles.org, www.baldeagleinfo.com, www.bbc.co.uk/nature, www.BBC.net, www.borealforest.org, www.britain-express.com, www.thebritishmuseum.ac.uk, www.burningman.com, www.centralparknyc.org, www.circlemakers.org, www.collectionscanada.ca, www.decadevolcano.net, www.dicamillocom-panion.com, www.dinercity.com, www.domebergland.co.za, www.edenproject.com, www.easternct.edu/depts/amerst/Malls.htm, http://edition.cnn.com, www.emporis.com/en, www.english-heritage.org.uk, www.escapeartist.com, www.everestnews.com, www.exploroz.com, www.extremescience.net, www.filmsite.org, www.forbestraveler.com, www.forestry.gov.uk, www.fosterandpartners.com, www.frommers.com, www.gbrmpa.gov.au, www.gibraltar.gov.gi, www.glasgowmuseums.com, www.goeurope.about.com, www.gonomad.com, http://gotorussia.vand.ru, www.greatbuildings.com, www.greatrailuk.com, www.greenpeace.org.uk, www.gumball3000.com, www.haliburtonforest.com, www.hearstcastle.org, www.ifyouski.com, www.hermitagemuseum.org, www.hkdolphinwatch.com, www.hummingbirds.net, www.imdb.com, www.ippar.pt, www.islamiccity.com, www.kew.org, www.landmarktrust.org.uk, www.lonelyplanet.com, www.manrecap.com, www.maizemaze.com, www.missbellowsfallsdiner.com, www.mooseworld.com, www.moretonbayislands.com.au, www.metmuseum.org, www.movie-locations.com, www.national-geographic.com, www.nationaltrust.org.uk, http://news.bbc.co.uk, www.nps.gov/parks.html, www.nytimes.com/pages/travel/index.html, www.panamacanalmuseum.org, www.pbs.org/science, www.peacemaze.com, www.piratesinfo.com, www.playbillarts.com, www.rspb.org.uk, www.projetoboto.com,www.pps.net.au/4wdencounter/readtrips/gunbarrel.html, www.rajasthan-tourism.gov.in, www.rarebreeds.co.nz, www.responsibletravel.com, www.roadsideamerica.com, www.ronemmons.com, www.rose-festival.com, www.royalparks.gov.uk, www.savethemanatee.org, www.scotsman.com, www.snopes.com, www.space-2001.net, www.spanish-fiestas.com, www.stan-leysubmarines.com, www.stellamarisdiving.com, www.stonehenge.co.uk, www.svalbard.com, www.taj-mahal.net, www.tate.org.uk, www.telegraph.co.uk, www.titanic-nautical.com, www.todossantos-baja.com, www.topiarygarden.org, http://travel.discovery.com, www.unb.ca, http://travel.independent.co.uk, http://travel.theemiratesnetwork.com, http://travel.timesonline.co.uk, www.turkeytravelplanner.com, www.undiscoveredscotland.co.uk, www.unesco.org, www.unusualho-telsoftheworld.com, http://vancouver.ca, www.volcanoes.com, http://volcano.und.edu, www.western-australia.com, www.wordsworth.org.uk, www.world-waterfalls.com, www.who.int, www.wikipedia.org, www.wikitravel.org, www.wolftrust.org.uk, www.wvbridgeday.com, www.wwf.org.uk, www.yukoninfo.com

Index